791.4372
I 29
2004

THE SHOOTING SCRIPT

I ♥ HUCKABEES

WRITTEN BY **DAVID O. RUSSELL** & **JEFF BAENA**

INTRODUCTION BY **DAVID O. RUSSELL**

Q&A WITH **DAVID O. RUSSELL**

D1122580

A Newmarket Shooting Script® Series Book
NEWMARKET PRESS • NEW YORK

FIRST EDITION

10   9   8   7   6   5   4   3   2   1

ISBN: 1-55704-656-5

Library of Congress Catalog-in-Publication Data is available upon request.

QUANTITY PURCHASES

Companies, professional groups, clubs, and other organizations may qualify for special terms when ordering quantities
of this title. For information, write to Special Sales, Newmarket Press, 18 East 48th Street, New York, NY 10017;
call (212) 832-3575 or 1-800-669-3903; FAX (212) 832-3629; or e-mail mailbox@newmarketpress.com.

Website: www.newmarketpress.com

Manufactured in the United States of America.

OTHER BOOKS IN THE NEWMARKET SHOOTING SCRIPT® SERIES INCLUDE:

About a Boy: The Shooting Script

Adaptation: The Shooting Script

The Age of Innocence: The Shooting Script

American Beauty: The Shooting Script

Ararat: The Shooting Script

A Beautiful Mind: The Shooting Script

Big Fish: The Shooting Script

The Birdcage: The Shooting Script

Blackhawk Down: The Shooting Script

Cast Away: The Shooting Script

Dead Man Walking: The Shooting Script

Dreamcatcher: The Shooting Script

Erin Brockovich: The Shooting Script

Eternal Sunshine of the Spotless Mind:
    The Shooting Script

Gods and Monsters: The Shooting Script

Gosford Park: The Shooting Script

Human Nature: The Shooting Script

The Ice Storm: The Shooting Script

Igby Goes Down: The Shooting Script

Knight's Tale: The Shooting Script

Man on the Moon: The Shooting Script

The Matrix: The Shooting Script

Nurse Betty: The Shooting Script

Pieces of April: The Shooting Script

The People vs. Larry Flynt: The Shooting Script

Punch-Drunk Love: The Shooting Script

Red Dragon: The Shooting Script

The Shawshank Redemption: The Shooting Script

Sideways: The Shooting Script

Snatch: The Shooting Script

Snow Falling on Cedars: The Shooting Script

State and Main: The Shooting Script

Sylvia: The Shooting Script

Traffic: The Shooting Script

The Truman Show: The Shooting Script

OTHER NEWMARKET PICTORIAL MOVIEBOOKS AND NEWMARKET INSIDER FILM BOOKS
INCLUDE:

The Age of Innocence: A Portrait of the Film★

Ali: The Movie and The Man★

Amistad: A Celebration of the Film by Steven Spielberg

The Art of The Matrix★

The Art of X2★

Bram Stoker's Dracula: The Film and the Legend★

Catch Me If You Can: The Illustrated Screenplay★

Chicago: The Movie and Lyrics★

Cold Mountain: The Journey from Book to Film

Crouching Tiger, Hidden Dragon: A Portrait of the Ang Lee Film★

Dances with Wolves: The Illustrated Story of the Epic Film★

E.T. The Extra Terrestrial From Concept to Classic—The
    Illustrated Story of the Film and the Filmmakers★

Frida: Bringing Frida Kahlo's Life and Art to Film★

Gladiator: The Making of the Ridley Scott Epic Film

Gods and Generals: The Illustrated Story of the Epic Civil War
    Film★

The Hulk: The Illustrated Screenplay★

In America: A Portrait of the Film★

The Jaws Log

Kinsey: Public and Private ★

Planet of the Apes: Re-imagined by Tim Burton★

Ray: A Tribute to the Movie, the Music and the Man★

Saving Private Ryan: The Men, The Mission, The Movie

The Sense and Sensibility Screenplay & Diaries★

Stuart Little: The Art, the Artists and the Story Behind the
    Amazing Movie★

Van Helsing: The Making of the Legend

★Includes Screenplay

CONTENTS

INTRODUCTION

BY DAVID O. RUSSELL

In 1990 I wrote a short film about a man who concealed microphones on every table in a Chinese restaurant, enabling him to eavesdrop and write insanely personal fortunes that eventually involve him in several people's lives. This was the first time I tried to write about a kind of existential detective. When I was fortunate enough to get grants from both the New York State Council on the Arts and the National Endowment for the Arts to make this short, I tried to grow it into a feature, but wasn't entirely happy with the results. I made *Spanking the Monkey* instead, which had been my side project while working on the fortune cookie feature.

Ten years later, I saw Jason Schwartzman in *Rushmore*, which I loved. Feeling he was a kindred spirit, I sought him out and we became good friends. I wrote a script for Jason and my friends Mark Wahlberg and Lily Tomlin that centered around a zendo, or zen center, I had gone to for four years in Manhattan. Each evening at six, stockbrokers, carpenters, janitors, scientists, all kinds of people would regularly arrive at this East Side townhouse, take off their coats, and sit in silence together, investigating consciousness and being—which I thought was funny, as well as serious.

The setting was ideal for a comedy about questions that had interested me for many years, dating to when I read J. D. Salinger's *Franny and Zooey* in high school and then took the classes of Indo-Tibetan scholar Robert Thurman in college. I wrote this zendo comedy for eighteen months after *Three Kings* was released, and then, though it was filled with things I loved, I concluded the film wasn't ready, which made for difficult calls to Jason, Mark, Lily, and Téa Leoni. I put the script in a drawer.

A week later I had a dream in which I was being followed by a woman detective, but not for criminal reasons, for spiritual reasons. I thought this was funny, and I felt this was the idea to make into a movie. This is the script that became *I ♥ Huckabees*, which I finished with my fellow investigator Jeff Baena.

People ask how I pitched such an idea to the studio. Like this: "Dustin Hoffman and Lily Tomlin are existential detectives whom you hire to investigate the meaning of your life at this moment. Their clients include Jason Schwartzman, Mark Wahlberg, Jude Law, and Naomi Watts. Their nemesis is Isabelle Huppert. Hilarity ensues."

To me the movie is about some of my favorite kind of people—those willing to follow a question or a cause to far reaches, regardless of convention. To quote Tommy Corn (Mark Wahlberg's character), "Why is it that people only ask themselves deep questions when something really bad happens, and then they forget all about it later, and how come people are so self destructive, and third, I refuse to use petroleum, and there's no way I can stop its use in my lifetime, is there? I mean Jimmy Carter would have a great electric car by now. I could have a Cadillac Escalade and it would be electric. I wouldn't have to ride my bicycle."

Or to quote Albert Markovski (Jason Schwartzman's character), "If the forms of this world die, which is more real, the me that dies or the me that's infinite? Can I trust my habitual mind or should I try to look beneath those things?" To which the young girl replies, "We don't have to ask those questions, do we, mom?" and Jean Smart warmly answers, "No, honey."

In this world, where the Brad Stands are at first glance the most charming, accessible, attractive and easy to side with, acting off basic assumptions and fears becomes standard versus challenging them. Public figures in the media use what is most reductive to get people's attention, which leaves little room for inquiry.

Jason's character is based on myself in my twenties, when I was an activist for better low-income housing and education in Maine and Boston. His friendship with Mark Wahlberg's character is based in some ways on my own unlikely but close friendship with Mark. We come from very different backgrounds and yet we are able to be very frank with each other about many personal and spiritual things. It is an enormous gift for a director when he knows an actor personally and sees comedy, emotion, and depth in him that have not yet been revealed in a film.

Somewhat similarly, neither Jude Law, with whom I have shared several dinners over the years, nor Naomi Watts, whom I adored in *Mulholland Drive*, had ever done a comedy. In the very year that they were anointed as golden icons with Oscar nominations and glamorous press, they both relished the opportunity to turn such icons on their heads through their characters in *Huckabees*.

Perhaps the most perfect thing about Isabelle Huppert joining the cast, beyond her dark complexity, intelligence, and sexiness, is that twenty-three years ago she held Jason Schwartzman in her arms as an infant while visiting her friend Talia Shire (Jason's mother), and now she would be rolling in the mud with him.

When Dustin Hoffman agreed to play Lily's husband and co-detective, I could not have been happier. He is probably the reason I got into cinema in the first place, having seen *The Graduate* when I was fifteen and holding it somewhere in my heart ever since, or feeling like it was already there before I even saw it. Dustin's first request was that I come to his home and read the script to him out loud so he could hear it the way I hear and feel it. This took two days, as we stopped and spoke many times about many things. My wish was to have a cast that shared my enthusiasm for questions about being, as well as a sense of humor about these questions. I was very lucky in getting this cast and we had an enormous amount of fun working together.

The blessing of being able to work with composer and songwriter Jon Brion, in addition to my trusted team of editors, continued the spirit of the film to the very end of making it. Philosophy interests me only insofar as it is practical and makes people feel more alive and open, not closed. I knew that making this film was a bit of a "Geronimo" leap, but I was sustained by my actors and crew and how close to my heart the characters and questions of the film are.

People sometimes ask me what the film is saying or what it means, and I can only say that the response I have heard that is closest to the film's intention is when people see it and feel a kind of elation at the end, combined with a thoughtfulness and wondering.

I ♥ HUCKABEES

Written by David O. Russell & Jeff Baena

Final Shooting Script

EXT. AN OPEN MEADOW - DAY

Out of focus at first, so that it looks like dots or grain --
and from this emerges, ALBERT, walking toward us, from about
100 yards off. We hear him speaking to himself, full volume,
like V.O.

                    ALBERT (V.O.)
          Motherfucking cocksucker,
          motherfucking shit fucker, what am
          I doing? I don't know what I'm
          doing, I'm doing the best that I
          can. I know that's all I can ask
          of myself. Is that good enough?
          Is my work doing any good? Is
          anybody paying attention? Is it
          hopeless to try to change things?
          The African guy is a sign, right?
          Because if he isn't, then nothing
          in this world makes any sense to
          me, I'm fucked. Maybe I should
          quit, don't quit. Maybe I should
          just fucking quit, don't fucking
          quit. I don't know what the fuck
          I'm supposed to fucking do anymore.
          Fucker, fuck, shit!

HE ARRIVES AT CAMERA, STOPS.

                    ALBERT (READS) (CONT'D)
          I'm glad we saved a piece of this
          marsh. I know it's small but at
          least it's something. Don't stop
          fighting. We're going to save a
          lot more of this place. To
          celebrate I have a poem I'd like to
          read. "Nobody sits like this rock
          sits, you rock, rock, the rock just
          sits and is, you show us how to
          just sit here, and that's what we
          need." (applause)

PAN to ROCK, about size of a third of a car, cordoned off
with yellow police tape, as construction workers with
surveying tape are all around preparing for construction in
the meadow, and a bulldozer stands by.

                    CROWD (APPLAUSE)
          Yeah! We did it!

                    ALBERT
          Did any press come?

(CONTINUED)

CONTINUED:

                    HARRISON
          The local paper. What's wrong?

                    ALBERT
          Nothing. I have an appointment to
          check out this African guy.

                    HARRISON
          What African guy?

                    ALBERT
          Exactly, what African guy?

EXT. ROUTE 4 - DAY

ALBERT MARKOVSKI, 21, wearing a dark suit, pin-striped shirt,
rides his bicycle through TRAFFIC.

EXT. SUBURBAN OFFICE BUILDING - DAY

He jumps off the bicycle in a hurry, locks it in front of a
modern office building.

INT. LOBBY OF OFFICE BUILDING - CONTINUOUS

He rushes into the lobby, glances at a business card in his
hand, scans the building directory of dentists, accountants,
JAFFE & JAFFE SUITE 909. He darts into an elevator.

INT. NINTH FLOOR HALL - CONTINUOUS

Albert walks fast down the corridor, past office doors,
around corner after corner in a labyrinthine series of
hallways. He finally comes to 909, and enters. MUSIC AND
CREDITS END.

INT. RECEPTION AREA - JAFFE AND JAFFE - CONTINUOUS

He walks into the reception area and up to the receptionist,
BOBBY, in a three-piece suit.

                    ALBERT
          Markovski, one o'clock, sorry I'm
          late. This place is like a maze.

                    BOBBY (SMILING)
          Have a seat, we'll be right with
          you.

                                              (CONTINUED)

CONTINUED:

Albert sits next to a WOMAN WITH A NINE-YEAR-OLD BOY, TWO MEN
holding hands. ALBERT DOES A DOUBLE TAKE ON AN AFRICAN MAN.

INT. VIVIAN'S OFFICE - DAY

A spare modern office with a large orange and blue color
field painting. Albert paces across from VIVIAN JAFFE, an
attractive, dark-haired, European-looking woman, 55, dressed
in a St. Laurent suit, with her feet up on her desk, her
hands clasped behind her head. She watches Albert as he
PACES, distraught, leans his head to the wall, upset.

                    VIVIAN
          Why don't you just tell me what
          your situation is?

                    ALBERT
          I don't even understand what you
          do.

                    VIVIAN (SIGHS)
          We'll investigate and solve your
          case.

                    ALBERT
          How?

                    VIVIAN
          If you sign a contract, we'll
          follow you.

                    ALBERT
          You'll spy.

                    VIVIAN
          Yes.

                    ALBERT
          On me.

                    VIVIAN
          Yes.

                    ALBERT
          When I'm going to the bathroom?

                    VIVIAN
          Yes.

                    ALBERT
          Why?

CONTINUED:

                    VIVIAN
          No thing can ever be too small. You
          know how the police can find the
          tiniest piece of DNA and build a
          case, we might see the way you
          floss or masturbate and it could be
          the key to your entire reality.

                    ALBERT
          So I'm hiring you to spy on me.

                    VIVIAN
          That's right, so we can figure out
          your case and solve your crisis. In
          addition, my associate will
          approach your case from a different
          angle.

                    ALBERT
          What angle?

                    VIVIAN
          Regarding your perception of
          reality. He'll talk to you about
          that. Who sent you here?

                    ALBERT (SHOWS CARD)
          Nobody. I found one of your cards.

                    VIVIAN
          Where?

                    ALBERT
          It was at a fancy restaurant I'd
          never been to.

MOS FLASHBACK - INT. FANCY RESTAURANT - DAY

The maître d' helps Albert put on the loaner jacket. Albert
puts his hands in the jacket's pocket and pulls out a
BUSINESS CARD.

                    ALBERT (V.O.)
          I didn't have the proper attire, so
          they let me borrow a suit jacket. I
          reached into the pocket and there
          was your card.

CLOSE UP on card: "JAFFE & JAFFE, CRISIS INVESTIGATION &
RESOLUTION."

CONTINUED:

                    ALBERT (V.O.) (CONT'D)
          The weird thing is I always wear a
          jacket.

                    VIVIAN (V.O.)
          But not that day.

                    ALBERT (V.O.)
          No.

Albert shakes hands with Brad, who is O.S. next to camera.

                    BRAD (O.S.)
          Brad Stand.

                    ALBERT
          Hey. (shakes Brad's hand)

BACK TO VIVIAN'S OFFICE

                    VIVIAN
          Kind of a coincidence.

                    ALBERT
          My case is a coincidence.

                    VIVIAN
          With the restaurant and the jacket?

                    ALBERT
          No, no, no. I'm talking about a big
          coincidence. It involves one man.
          It has three parts. OK, ready?

Vivian listens.

                    ALBERT (CONT'D)
          One, I was at Schottinger's Photo
          Archive, it was my first time
          there. I wanted an early Bob Dylan
          photo, because I like Bob Dylan.

MOS FLASHBACK: ALBERT WATCHES THE AFRICAN MAN FLIP THROUGH
PHOTOS AT SCHOTTINGER'S. THEY SPEAK TO EACH OTHER AS
PROPRIETOR BIK SCHOTTINGER SITS IN THE BACKGROUND.

                    ALBERT (V.O.)
          -- and in comes this tall African
          guy, about 18 years old or something.
          You know, he's in there getting
          glossies of Samuel L. Jackson,

                                        (CONTINUED)

CONTINUED:

>   Shaquille O'Neal, Jim Carrey. He's
>   an autograph hound. The kind of guy
>   who likes to get glossies of famous
>   people and get them signed --

BACK TO

>   ALBERT (CONT'D)
>   Two weeks later I see the same tall
>   African guy who's working as a
>   doorman at my friend's building.

MOS FLASHBACK: THE AFRICAN MAN IS DRESSED IN A DOORMAN'S
UNIFORM AT A RESIDENTIAL BUILDING. ALBERT STARES AT HIM.

>   BACK TO:

>   VIVIAN (WRITING)
>   Who's the friend?

>   ALBERT
>   Jay Wendorff, but it's not his
>   apartment, it's his girlfriend's.

>   VIVIAN (WRITING)
>   What's her name?

>   ALBERT
>   Uh, Kelly Coulter. So that's two
>   parts, first at Schottinger's, then
>   the doorman. Now, third time, I see
>   him in a car at the mall.

>   VIVIAN
>   What were you doing there?

>   ALBERT
>   Working.

>   CUT TO:

ALBERT FINISHES PLANTING A TREE IN A TRAFFIC LANE, PAN BACK
TO ALBERT AND HIS TREE AS A MINI-VAN SCREECHES TO A STOP IN
FRONT OF THE TREE.

>   ALBERT (V.O.)(CONT'D)
>   I'm making a statement for the Open
>   Spaces. I planted a tree in the
>   traffic lane.

>   ALBERT (CONT'D)
>   OH MY GOD!

CONTINUED:

                    SECURITY GUARD
          You don't plant no tree here.

Albert stares at the AFRICAN MAN in the mini-van as the
Security Guard tackles Albert.

BACK TO VIVIAN'S OFFICE

They sit in silence for a moment. She swivels in her chair to
a row of large notebooks hand-labeled: DEATH, CONFUSIONS,
CONFLICTS, WARS, MOTHERS, FATHERS, COINCIDENCES, LOVE,
GALAXIES. She pulls COINCIDENCES.

                    VIVIAN
          They're not always meaningful.

                    ALBERT
          Yeah, it's meaningful.

                    VIVIAN
          About your life?

                    ALBERT
          Yeah, my life. And about the whole
          thing. The universe you know. The
          big one. Should I keep doing what
          I'm doing or stop because it's
          hopeless?

                    VIVIAN (SIGHS)
          Mr. Markovski, we see a lot of
          people in here who claim they want
          to know the ultimate truth about
          reality, they want to peer under
          the surface at the big everything,
          but that can be a painful process
          full of surprises. It can dismantle
          the world as you know it. For this
          reason, many people prefer to stay
          on the surface of things. Maybe you
          should go home, let sleeping dogs
          lie, take it easy, what do you say?

                    ALBERT
          I say don't give me the brush-off.
          Please.

                    VIVIAN (SCRUTINIZING HIM)
          Have you ever transcended space and
          time?

CONTINUED:

> ALBERT
> Yes... No... I don't know what
> you're talking about.

> VIVIAN
> I take it you don't make much
> money, Mr. Markovski?

> ALBERT
> Ahhh, no. Is it expensive, what you
> do here?

> VIVIAN (WRITING)
> Mmmm. We have a sliding scale, some
> of our clients pay thirty dollars a
> week, and we have wealthy clients
> who pay several thousand a week.

> ALBERT
> I can't believe you even exist. How
> long have you been doing this?

> VIVIAN
> Seventeen years, 342 cases.

> ALBERT
> I'm gonna have to ask you to steer
> clear of my office because my job
> situation's a little shaky.

> VIVIAN
> You want us to stay away from your
> job?

> ALBERT
> Yeah, if you come snooping around
> my office, it could make me look
> unstable and it could hurt me.

> VIVIAN
> I want you to meet my colleague.

She stands, opens the door to the next office, Albert
follows.

INT. BERNARD'S OFFICE - CONTINUOUS

BERNARD JAFFE, 60, intellectual, disheveled, but elegant in a
suit, sits at his desk working on shards of china in dirt.

9.

CONTINUED:

                    VIVIAN
          Bernard, this is Mr. Markovski,
          he's gonna have to be pro bono.

Bernard stands, shakes Albert's hand, wheels out a table with
a BODY-SIZED BLACK GORTEX COCOON ON IT.

                    VIVIAN (CONT'D)
          Hold on, he hasn't signed a
          contract.

                    BERNARD
          Let me do this. Then we'll get to
          the contract --

          VIVIAN   BERNARD
No, it's too much too soon --   It's always too much too
                                soon, that's the nature of
                                the beast --

          VIVIAN   BERNARD
Approach, patience, finesse -- Will you stop?

                    VIVIAN
          We need to begin with his
          specifics.

                    BERNARD
          But we need to go past logic.

She smooches him quickly, it turns into a longer kiss, some
caressing while Albert watches. Then Vivian withdraws.

                    BERNARD (CONT'D)
          Where are we going for dinner?

                    VIVIAN
          Korean barbecue.

                    BERNARD
          Really?

Albert and Bernard are alone. BERNARD PULLS OUT A LARGE WHITE
BLANKET, OPENS IT.

                    BERNARD (CONT'D)
          Let's get started.

                    ALBERT
          Is this part of my investigation?

(CONTINUED)

CONTINUED: (2)

> BERNARD (HOLDS BLANKET OPEN)
> Yes. Let's say that this blanket
> represents all the matter and
> energy in the universe, OK?

> ALBERT
> OK.

> BERNARD
> All the particles, everything.

> ALBERT
> What's outside the blanket?

> BERNARD
> More blankets, that's the point.

> ALBERT
> OK.

> BERNARD
> Just say this is everything. And
> here --

HE HOLDS HIS HAND UNDER THE BLANKET, MAKING A LITTLE PUPPET.

> BERNARD (CONT'D)
> This is me, see? I'm sixty
> something years old, I'm wearing a
> suit, blah blah. And over here,
> this is you, you're, I don't know,
> twenty-one, dark hair, etcetera --

He makes another hand puppet from under the blanket.

> BERNARD (MAKING MANY BLANKET PUPPETS)
> (CONT'D)
> And over here, this is Vivian. And
> here, this is Paris, and this is a
> war, and this is a museum, and this
> is a disease, and this is an
> orgasm, and this is a hamburger --
> get it?

> ALBERT
> Everything's the same thing, even
> if it's different.

> BERNARD
> Exactly. But our everyday mind
> forgets this.
> (MORE)

(CONTINUED)

CONTINUED: (3)

                    BERNARD (CONT'D)
          We think everything is separate,
          limited, you're over there, I'm
          over here, which is true...but not
          the whole truth.

                    ALBERT
          OK.

                    BERNARD
          Good. So, we need to learn how to
          see the blanket truth all the time,
          right in the everyday stuff, and
          that's what this is for.

He dramatically, loudly, UNZIPS the GORTEX COCOON for Albert.

                    ALBERT
          Why?

                    BERNARD
          Why what?

                    ALBERT
          Why do we need to learn how to see
          the unity-blanket thing all the
          time?

                    BERNARD
          Well. You wouldn't want to miss out
          on the big picture, would you?

                    ALBERT
          No.

                    BERNARD
          Also, it helps.

                    ALBERT
          How?

                    BERNARD
          When you get the blanket thing, you
          can relax, because everything you
          could ever want or be, you already
          have and are. Does that sound good?

                    ALBERT (LOOKING AT THE COCOON)
          Very good.

                    BERNARD
          OK, get in.

CONTINUED: (4)

                    ALBERT
          So....get in here?

                    BERNARD
          Uh huh.

Albert climbs into the cocoon. Bernard zips it shut.

                    BERNARD (CONT'D)
          The purpose of this suit, Mr.
          Markovski, is to help shut down
          your everyday perceptions and give
          up your usual identity that
          separates you from everything: your
          body, your senses, your name, your
          job, everything you identify with,
          your family, this room, this
          street, this town, this country,
          this economy, this history, this
          planet, the things you think make
          you separate, let them all go.

EXT. COCOON

Bernard stands looking at his watch, pours himself a glass of
water and eats a cracker slowly.

INT. ALBERT'S MIND - CONTINUOUS

Albert's breathing is the only sound in the blackness, and
now, IMAGES OF WHAT HE'S THINKING APPEAR: Wide shot of the
room, the black cocoon on the table. The office melts away,
revealing a cityscape outside, which melts, then a horizon
POV of the USA, which melts, then the planet, which melts.
Till Albert, fading in and out, appears standing before a
grey/blue background.

The magnified head of BRAD STAND, a blond, corporate stud,
appears.

                    BRAD'S HEAD (FRIENDLY)
          Hey, man, how's it going? (He
          laughs) You're an asshole.

The head of DARLENE, a plain secretary, joins Brad's head.

                    DARLENE'S HEAD
          We will destroy you.

The head of the African refugee appears, with a Shaq glossy.

CONTINUED:

                    MR. NIMIERI'S HEAD (WITH ACCENT)
          I got Shaq!

FLASHBACK: DINNER WITH BRAD

                    ALBERT
          I think you guys can rebuild in
          areas that are run down, instead of
          tearing up new land.

                    BRAD
          Definitely. We're open to that.

                    ALBERT
          This is who we are at Open Spaces,
          we can't throw that away --

                    BRAD
          Well, look, I'm not gonna bullshit
          you, right? I mean, part of it is
          we've taken a beating in the press
          about all our growth, opening so
          many stores in such a short time,
          not caring about the communities
          we're in -- so if we work with you
          and your Open Spaces Coalition,
          does this help the Huckabees image?
          Yes. Does it help me? Yes. Does it
          benefit me if I bring some great PR
          to Huckabees when we need it?
          Absolutely. But do I also care
          about saving open space? Yes. Do I
          also like to get outside and have
          some peace and solitude, go
          mountain biking, go jet skiing?
          absofuckinglutely. Do I love Dylan?
          Are you kidding me? Do I dig your
          poems? Do I have to say it again?
          So why can't it all work together
          for a good end?

                    ALBERT
          Also if we're gonna work together,
          you guys have to commit to using
          recycled bags --

                    BRAD
          Mmmmm.

A seventies' bathing-suit still of Jessica Lange floats into
view over flashback.

CONTINUED:

                    JESSICA LANGE STILL
              Ohhhh...Albert.

She MORPHS into DAWN CAMPBELL, a young Barbie blond, removing
her clothes.

                    DAWN
              Stop looking at me, what's wrong
              with you? Stop looking at me...

ANGELA FRANCO, 60, City Councilwoman, appears.

                    ANGELA'S HEAD
              BEAT IT, you little pussy.

BERNARD UNZIPS THE SUIT, ALBERT SITS UP, FLUSTERED.

                    ALBERT (SHAKING, SWEATING)
              Whoa. You said that would relax me.

                    BERNARD (PATTING ALBERT ON THE BACK)
              Eventually. Practice at home.

                    ALBERT
              I don't have one of these.

                    BERNARD
              Try it wherever you are. Use an eye
              mask, or just close your eyes.

INT. ALBERT'S BATHROOM - THE NEXT DAY

Albert lays in his bathtub, eyes covered in a black mask.

Albert brushes his teeth, unaware that Vivian peers through
the window from the fire escape, writing notes.

INT. ALBERT'S SMALL LIVING ROOM/DINING ROOM - A BIT LATER

Albert sits eating a bowl of cereal and NOTICES VIVIAN spying
from the fire escape.

                    ALBERT (THROUGH THE WINDOW GLASS)
              What should I be doing?

                    VIVIAN (THROUGH THE WINDOW GLASS)
              Whatever you normally do.

Albert resumes eating, a bit self-consciously. He glances up
at VIVIAN who nods and motions for Albert to continue.

EXT. ALBERT'S BUILDING - SUBURB - DAY

Albert exits his small apartment building with his bike.
VIVIAN follows on her bike.

EXT. ROUTE 4 - DAY

Albert rides his bike along Route 4, a lone pedestrian next
to rushing cars. Vivian follows twenty feet behind.

EXT. LARGE MALL - DAY

MONTAGE SEQUENCE: Albert reads a poem in a parking lot.
Shoppers pass him: CONSTRUCTION WORKERS STOP AND LISTEN. They
throw food at him. One of them apologizes.

EXT. ROUTE 4 - LATER

Albert walks his bike along the heavily trafficked road,
tailed by Vivian as cars zip past.

EXT. OPEN SPACES COALITION OFFICES, STRIP MALL - LATER

Albert goes into his office, a small storefront in a strip
mall, Vivian watches. ACROSS THE STREET, A MYSTERIOUS ELEGANT
BLOND FRENCH WOMAN, 47, CATERINE VAUBAN, stands watching.

INT. COALITION OFFICE - CONTINUOUS

It's a neat campaign office: two simple desks, a table
covered with petitions; a large poster of Henry David
Thoreau; a photograph of a forest and marsh. Vivian watches
Albert through the glass store front as he listens to a
MESSAGE MACHINE.

                    WOMAN ON MESSAGE MACHINE
              "I wanted to thank you for what you
              did with the oak tree in Miller's
              Square. I played on that tree when
              I was a little girl. I thought we
              had a chance but they chopped it--"
              Beep.

VIVIAN COMES INSIDE THE OFFICE, PULLS A SURVEILLANCE BUG FROM
HER BAG, PLACES IT ON THE TELEPHONE, another on the wall, and
another on the ceiling. Albert inspects one of the
surveillance mikes. Vivian exits.

EXT. OPEN SPACES COALITION OFFICE, STRIP MALL - DAY

Vivian sits on a bench and pulls out headphones from her
purse, pulling up an antenna. She listens to Albert inside as
TWO COLLEGE GUYS, HARRISON and TIM, WALK IN and talk to him.

>   ALBERT (O.S.)
>   Hey, what's going on? Where is
>   everyone?

>   HARRISON (O.S.)
>   Brad moved the meeting.

INT. ALBERT'S OFFICE - CONTINUOUS

>   ALBERT
>   He what?

>   HARRISON
>   To Huckabees Corporate.

>   ALBERT   HARRISON
> All right, listen. Okay. I   OK, OK.
> want you to do this, I want
> you to get me the National
> Office on the phone right
> now, you call Orrin Spence
> and tell him that Brad Stand
> is trying to hijack my
> coalition. All right? Do
> that right now, please. And
> this should've gone out to
> the other chapter a week ago.

The door opens and COUNCILWOMAN ANGELA FRANCO, 60, comes in.

>   ANGELA FRANCO
>   I want your flyers out of that
>   parking lot.

>   ALBERT
>   It's a free country. Poems work.

>   ANGELA FRANCO
>   You're pissing people off.

>   ALBERT
>   My poems were supposed to go out
>   with the Shania mailing.

>   ANGELA FRANCO
>   Brad Stand is a businessman --

                                              (CONTINUED)

CONTINUED:

                    ALBERT
          Oh, please.

                    ANGELA FRANCO
          He knows how to be reasonable,
          you're not running this Coalition
          anymore.

                    ALBERT
          I'm still in the charter. I wrote
          it.

                    ANGELA FRANCO
          Not for long.

She leaves.

                    ALBERT
          I love these flyers.

                    HARRISON (HANGING UP PHONE)
          I can't get him. He's in a
          meeting.

                    ALBERT
          Can you just keep trying? Orrin
          Spence, Orrin Spence. Brad cannot
          do this to us, all right?

                    HARRISON
          How can she get you out of the
          charter, man?

                    ALBERT
          She can't!

Albert covertly speaks into one of the surveillance bugs.

                    ALBERT (SOTTO VOCE) (CONT'D)
          This is my work situation, the one
          I was telling you about. It's a
          little...I'll describe it to you
          later if you could just...

Vivian, wearing surveillance headphones, stares at Albert
through the glass storefront. The frosh guys look puzzled.

                    HARRISON
          Don't worry, Albert. We're going
          to knock that meeting on its ass.

Albert goes outside.

EXT. ALBERT'S STRIP MALL STOREFRONT OFFICE - DAY

Albert walks up to Vivian.

                    VIVIAN
          So you're fighting suburban sprawl,
          and this guy Brad Stand and you had
          some kind of a falling out --

                    ALBERT
          You're standing out like a sore
          thumb. Remember I told you not to
          come by my work situation?

                    VIVIAN
          Oh yes, I remember. Now tell me,
          did the Coalition inspire the
          poetry or did the poetry inspire
          the Coalition?

                    ALBERT
          This is looking a little weird
          right now. Can we schedule a time
          when you can come by?

                    VIVIAN
          You know this, this --

                    ALBERT
          This has nothing to do with my
          coincidence! My coincidence has
          to do with this tall African guy --

SUDDENLY A WHITE CITROEN PULLS UP AND BERNARD JUMPS OUT WITH
A CELL PHONE IN HIS HAND.

                    BERNARD (HANDS VIVIAN THE CELL PHONE)
          Mr. Corn is having a crisis, you
          better talk to him.

VIVIAN TAKES THE CELL PHONE.

                    VIVIAN (FRUSTRATED, TAKES THE CALL)
          Tommy? What is it?

She steps to the side and talks on the phone.

                    BERNARD (TO ALBERT)
          OK, catch me up to speed. Tell me
          what's happening.

                                              (CONTINUED)

CONTINUED:

                    ALBERT
         What's happening is she wants to
         talk to me about my work situation
         and I want to talk about my
         coincidence.

                    BERNARD
         I'm talking about what's happening
         right now.

                    ALBERT
         This is what's happening right now.
         I'm telling you. She's spying --

                    BERNARD
         I'm talking about the blanket.

                    ALBERT
         I don't know how to do the blanket
         right now.

                    BERNARD
         Like this.

Bernard and Albert stare at each other for a few moments.
ALBERT, BERNARD, and the shapes around them VIBRATE INTO
SMALL SQUARES COMPOSING THEM.

                    VIVIAN
         Whoa, what are you doing? I need
         facts to piece together a theory.

The spell is broken. ALBERT LOOKS slightly freaked out.

                    BERNARD (VULNERABLE)
         Oh, no time for infinity. Gotta
         piece together a theory.

                    ALBERT
         This isn't cool.

                    VIVIAN (TO BERNARD)
         Listen, you go visit Mr. Corn. His
         wife is leaving him. I think I've
         got a really hot lead, Bernard.

                    BERNARD
         Albert, the universe is an infinite
         sphere whose center is everywhere
         and circumference is nowhere.

CONTINUED: (2)

                    ALBERT
          How can the center be --

He freezes mid-sentence when HE SEES VIVIAN RUN ACROSS THE
PARKING LOT, DIVE THROUGH THE WINDOW OF A PARKED RED BUICK.
Angela Franco walks by eating an ice cream cone and gets into
the red Buick. SHE DRIVES OFF, WITH VIVIAN HIDDEN IN THE BACK
SEAT. Albert watches the car drive off, freaked out.

               ALBERT (STUNNED) (CONT'D)
          She just dove into the back of
          Angela's car.

               BERNARD (CHECKS WATCH)
          You know you've gotta keep using
          the method, Albert. I gotta check
          in on Mr. Corn right now, OK?

Bernard hurries to his Citroen.

INT. ANGELA FRANCO'S RED BUICK - DAY

               ANGELA FRANCO (LICKING HER ICE CREAM)
          Um num num mm um num numm.

Vivian lays on the floor of the back seat, listening.

EXT. TOMMY CORN'S WORKING CLASS RANCH HOUSE - DAY

FOUR FIREMEN move furniture out of TOMMY CORN'S house, into a
U-HAUL truck, as TOMMY'S WIFE, Molly, MOVES OUT with their
six-year-old, CAITLIN. TOMMY CORN, a fireman, 31, wears
pajamas and fireman boots, chasing them.

               TOMMY CORN (PULLS HER BAG AWAY)
          Don't, baby, come on, don't do
          this --

               MOLLY (PULLS BAG BACK)
          You don't need anyone.

               TOMMY CORN
          That's not true, I need you.

               MOLLY
          If nothing matters, how can I
          matter?

               TOMMY CORN
          Let's figure it out --

                                              (CONTINUED)

                          MOLLY
          LET GO OF ME.

                          BERNARD (WALKS UP)
          Can we talk for a second here?

                          MOLLY
          Not you again.

She goes back to loading her car.

                          BERNARD (TO TOMMY)
          Calm down, tell me what happened.

                          TOMMY CORN
          She won't stay and share this with
          me and it's important, I see it so
          clearly.

                          BERNARD
          We've been over this.

                          TOMMY CORN
          By using petroleum, you're a
          murderer three times: killing the
          ozone and all the creatures that
          hurts; 2) killing the Arabs in oil-
          producing dictatorships where
          everyone is poor -- that is cruelty
          and it's inhumane.

                          MOLLY (LOADING CAR)
          WILL YOU STOP WITH THAT CRAP?

                          TOMMY CORN
          But then if this world is
          temporary, and identity is an
          illusion, then everything is
          meaningless, and it doesn't matter
          if we use petroleum, and that's got
          me very confused.

                          BERNARD
          It matters, it matters, look --

Bernard unfolds a map of the cosmos.

                          BERNARD (HOLDING COSMOS MAP) (CONT'D)
          Here's the universe, Tommy, we're
          over here in this galaxy of --

CONTINUED: (2)

                    TOMMY CORN
          What universe?

                    BERNARD
          This. The universe. Come on.

                    TOMMY CORN
          There's dust and gas out there, us
          over here, and good or bad luck.
          That's chaos. That's my B).

                    BERNARD
          This doesn't sound like you.

Tommy pulls a book from his pocket: "IF NOT NOW" by Caterine
Vauban. A PHOTO SHOWS THE MYSTERIOUS BLOND WHO TAILED ALBERT.

                    TOMMY CORN (OPENING BOOK)
          Vauban talks about space --

                    BERNARD (FREAKED OUT, TAKES IT)
          WHERE DID YOU GET THIS BOOK?

                    TOMMY CORN
          You sent it to me.

                    BERNARD (EXTREMELY UPSET)
          We would NEVER send you this book.

                    TOMMY CORN
          You didn't send this to me?

                    BERNARD
          No. Caterine Vauban is full of
          shit. What is she doing here? She
          never leaves Paris, this is insane.

                    TOMMY CORN
          It's a pretty good book. She says
          that nothing's connected, so you
          can do whatever you want, drive a
          car, burn up gas -- which would
          explain the way things actually
          are, where people do destructive
          things like it doesn't matter.

                    BERNARD (PISSED)
          There isn't an atom in our bodies
          that wasn't forged in the furnace
          of the sun. (READS) "Less than five
          percent of the cosmos" --

                                        (CONTINUED)

CONTINUED: (3)

Bernard sees Molly pass.

                BERNARD (CONT'D)
Molly, you can't leave Tommy in the
middle of his dismantling. He'll
never make it to the other side.

                MOLLY
I'm dying to stick around for his
dismantling.

                TOMMY CORN
You don't want to ask these
questions?

                MOLLY
I want to live my life.

                TOMMY CORN
But what is that life? What are we
part of? Who are we? Do you know
where these come from? (grabs
sneakers she's carrying)

                MOLLY
The store.

                TOMMY CORN (READING LABEL)
Indonesia. Little girls like you
(to his daughter) work in dark
factories where they go blind for a
dollar sixty a day, can you imagine
that, Caitlin?

                CAITLIN
I don't want the children to work
in factories --

                MOLLY
Daddy's crazy, honey, don't
listen --

                TOMMY CORN
Daddy's not crazy, the world is
crazy and it's important to --

Molly starts smacking him about the head and shoulders. A
fireman pulls Molly off Tommy, who goes back to Bernard.

(CONTINUED)

CONTINUED: (4)

>   TOMMY CORN (READING) (CONT'D)
>   "Less than five percent of the
>   cosmos is composed of the same
>   elements that compose human life."

>   FIREMAN
>   What does that matter?

>   TOMMY CORN
>   You should be asking these
>   questions, Skip.

>   FIREMAN 2
>   Tommy's very sensitive so his
>   therapist is here to hold his hand.

>   BERNARD
>   Excuse me, what did you call me?

>   FIREMAN 2
>   You're his therapist, right?

Tommy punches him in the jaw; the fireman goes down, lies
motionless while his friend tries to revive him. Without
missing a beat, Tommy turns back to Bernard with the book.

>   TOMMY CORN
>   We gotta sit down and talk because
>   this book is making a lot of sense
>   to me.

BERNARD NODS, WALKS BACK TO THE CITROEN MUTTERING TO HIMSELF.

>   BERNARD (MUTTERS TO HIMSELF)
>   What is Caterine Vauban doing in
>   the United States?

>   TOMMY CORN (YELLING AFTER BERNARD)
>   WHAT ARE YOU TALKING ABOUT?

EXT. HUCKABEES CORPORATE CENTER - DAY

Angela Franco walks through the large parking lot of a glass-
and-chrome corporate headquarters. Vivian follows 30 paces
behind as Angela enters. Caterine watches from a distance.

INT. HUCKABEES CORPORATE CENTER - DAY

EXPLOSIVE LAUGHTER from TEN PEOPLE in a small conference room
with a sales meeting underway. BRAD STAND, 31, is a tanned,
cock-of-the-walk, star sales director for the Target-like
retail chain Huckabees.

(CONTINUED)

CONTINUED:

                          BRAD
               You think that's funny. Listen to
               this.

Everyone laughs. VIVIAN enters laughing, plants a bug on the
door and exits.

                          BRAD (CONT'D)
               I've got a story for you that's
               only four months old.

          MARTY   DARLENE (LAUGHING)
Wait, wait, wait. Listen,   Oh, I love this one!
listen. Listen to the master,
all right?

JUST OUTSIDE THE DOOR, Vivian CROUCHES EAVESDROPPING.

                          BRAD (CONT'D)
               I'm with Shania, and we were
               opening up the megastore down by
               the loop. Shania's there to
               promote her apparel, right? It's
               four o'clock and she's starving, so
               I order a ton of tuna fish
               sandwiches, NO MAYO, Darlene --

                          DARLENE (PLAYFULY)
               Stop it!

Laughter.

                          BRAD
               Shania hates mayo. And she cannot
               eat chicken salad -- that's no
               joke. We once gave it to her and
               she threw up in the limo. The lady
               hates chicken salad. So we give
               her the tuna sandwiches but she
               doesn't believe there's no mayo in
               the tuna, swears she tastes it, so
               I tell her I'm allergic to mayo,
               which is a lie, and to prove it I
               eat two of the sandwiches in front
               of her; so now she eats one and a
               half, before she realizes... (he
               hesitates for an irrepressible
               chuckle) it's chicken salad, and
               she actually likes it!

Explosive laughter.

CONTINUED: (2)

>   MARTY
> She did not vomit. He made her
> change her mind. And that's what
> they want upstairs in corporate.
> OK?

>   DARLENE
> I'll be right back with those
> quarterlies.

EXT. BRAD'S CONFERENCE ROOM - HUCKABEES - CONTINUOUS

Darlene finds Vivian eavesdropping with headphones.

>   DARLENE (IRATE)
> Can I help you?

>   VIVIAN (WEARING HEADPHONES)
> I'm here for the Coalition meeting
> with Brad Stand.

>   DARLENE (IRATE)
> You have no reason to be here,
> dearie, I'm surprised they let you
> in, come with me.

She leads Vivian down the hall, past life-sized cardboard cut-
outs of Shania Twain promoting Huckabees, lots of offices.
CATERINE VAUBAN FOLLOWS THEM from a distance. They pass A
RECORDING STUDIO where COMMERCIALS are being recorded by DAWN
CAMPBELL, 30, THE SMOKY-VOICED ALL-AMERICAN BLOND WHO TAUNTED
ALBERT IN HIS MIND. SHE MOVES AND DANCES AS SHE TALKS.

INT. HUCKABEES RECORDING BOOTH - CONTINUOUS

>   DARYL
> OK, Dawn. Let's do another one.
> Stay loose. You're doing great.

>   DAWN (DANCING A LITTLE)
> "At Huckabees, the Everything
> Store." Let's do that one more
> time. I can't do this. OK. "Tops
> and mops, it's fifty percent off
> all women's shirts and hair
> products, this week only, at
> Huckabees, the Everything Store."

Vivian pauses to watch through the glass. Dawn looks
stressed, a bit unhappy.

CONTINUED:

                    DARYL
          Uh, Dawn? Can we do that one more
          time? I think we can do it better.

                    DAWN
          I suck, Daryl. That really sucked.
          I can't do this. I can't do it.

                    DARYL
          Don't give me that face. Your
          voice is the trademark voice of
          Huckabees.

OUTSIDE THE GLASS:

                    DARLENE (TO VIVIAN)
          Oh, there she is! You are one
          sneaky lady. I was almost in the
          elevators. We're going now. C'mon
          now. Let's move it along. There
          we go. Let's move it along. I'll
          show you where you need to go.
          This is the first time the Open
          Spaces Coalition is meeting here at
          Huckabees.

Darlene leads Vivian down the hall.

EXT. WOODS DURING FIRST COALITION MEETING AT HUCKABEES

Albert sits alone on the rock he saved. He sits, upset, folds
arms across his chest.

                    ALBERT (V.O.)
          Moved my meeting to the Huckabees
          Corporation. I saved this rock.
          I'm going to save this place.
          They're not going to save this
          place. Rat-fucking bastard Brad
          Stand! Corporate prick. Bastard.
          Motherfucking dickhead!

Albert writes in his journal.

                    ALBERT (V.O.)(CONT'D)
          Betrayed, by Albert Markovski. Is
          it possible for anyone in this
          world to work together to make it
          better? I don't think so.

CONTINUED:

> HARRISON (V.O.)
> It was Albert's vision. This whole
> thing was Albert's vision.

> VIVIAN (V.O.)
> Tell me about Brad Stand.

> HARRISON (V.O.)
> Well, Albert let him in. Which was
> a mistake.

> ALBERT
> Fuuuuuuuuuuuhhhhh!

> ANGELA (V.O.)
> He has been enormously helpful!

> HARRISON (V.O.)
> He dropped Albert's poems from the
> benefit!

> TIM (V.O.)
> And the mailing!

INT. HUCKABEES CORPORATE - GLASS CONFERENCE ROOM WITH A GROUP
OF COALITION MEMBERS INCLUDING: COUNCILWOMAN ANGELA FRANCO;
THE TWO GUY FROSHES HARRISON AND TIM, ARMS FOLDED DEFIANTLY;
TWO GIRL FROSHES; MARY JANE HUTCHINSON, AN ELDERLY WOMAN IN
RIDING ATTIRE.

> VIVIAN (O.S.)
> Settle down! Someone tell me about
> the woods and the marsh.

> ANGELA
> Mary Jane, it's your story, you
> tell it.

> MARY JANE HUTCHINSON
> All right. My great grandfather
> owned the woods and the marsh. We
> deeded them over to the municipal-
> ity in 1972 in perpetuity for the
> public.

> VIVIAN
> Tell me why.

CONTINUED:

> > MARY JANE HUTCHINSON
> > We just wanted to share this
> > beautiful place and now the town is
> > looking at subclauses and all of a
> > sudden wants yet another mall and
> > houses on this beautiful marsh.

> > HARRISON
> > So we're fighting it.

> > MARY JANE HUTCHINSON
> > We will fight it.

> > FROSH GIRLS
> > We have to save this marsh.

The door opens, Brad Stand enters with a large mounted photo
of a wetland with Shania Twain superimposed on top of it and
some Shania Twain T-shirts.

> > BRAD
> > Sorry I'm late, guys, got the photo
> > of our wetland right here. See, an
> > image is always better. You gotta
> > reach people quick. They have no
> > time for poems. They don't even
> > understand poems. They have to
> > think about it too much.

> > ANGELA FRANCO
> > Fantastic, Brad.

> > BRAD
> > Shania tees, extra small for your
> > grandson, Mary Jane.

> > MARY JANE HUTCHINSON
> > Bradley, you shouldn't have.

Everyone takes a "SHANIA FOR OPEN SPACES" T-shirt.

> FROSH GIRLS   ANGELA FRANCO
> YESS.   Fantastic, Bradley.

> > BRAD
> > Here's the schedule for the
> > benefit.
> > > (MORE)

CONTINUED: (2)

                    BRAD (CONT'D)
          First cocktails, then we open with
          the video about the marsh, then
          Angela, you give your speech, then
          Marty will speak for Huckabees.
          Then Shania sings! (HE LOOKS AT
          VIVIAN) Hi. Have we met?

                    ANGELA FRANCO
          I'm sorry, what is your name?

                    VIVIAN
          Vivian Jaffe.

                    ANGELA FRANCO
          She's a potential from ...

                    VIVIAN
          Albert Markovski.

     MARY JANE HUTCHINSON   ANGELA FRANCO
Oops.   Oh, no.

                    BRAD
          That's not gonna work, I'm sorry.
          How are you connected?

                    VIVIAN
          Through an investigation.

                    MARY JANE HUTCHINSON
          Oh, my.

                    BRAD
          See, I worry about that guy. What
          kind of investigation?

                    VIVIAN
          Existential. I'd like to ask some
          questions, if you don't mind.

                    BRAD
          Actually, we do, because we need to
          meet and we're late. I'm not trying
          to give you a hard time. Your work
          sounds very interesting. Have you
          got a card?

She hands Brad her card. Brad reads the BUSINESS CARD:
"VIVIAN JAFFE, EXISTENTIAL DETECTIVE, CRISIS
INVESTIGATION/RESOLUTION."

INT. BERNARD'S OFFICE - DAY

                    ALBERT (FURIOUS, PANICKED)
          I TOLD YOU TO STAY AWAY FROM MY
          WORK SITUATION.

                    VIVIAN
          If we're gonna solve your
          coincidence we have to put it into
          context. The conflict with Brad
          Stand seems very important.

                    ALBERT (ANGRY)
          So you show up at Huckabees
          Corporate and say you're my fucking
          existential detective? I'm lucky if
          I last another day.

                    VIVIAN
          We'll solve the case sooner if
          you're straight with us.

                    ALBERT
          I'm being straight with you. Brad
          smeared me and took the Coalition
          in another direction.

                    VIVIAN
          At Bik Schottinger's photo archive,
          where you met Mr. Nimieri --

                    ALBERT
          Who's that?

                    VIVIAN
          The African guy.

                    ALBERT
          That's the African guy from my
          coincidence. This is what I want
          to talk about.

                    VIVIAN
          It wasn't your first time at
          Schottinger's, was it?

                    ALBERT
          I wanna know about my coincidence.

                    VIVIAN
          It wasn't your first time, was it?

                                        (CONTINUED)

CONTINUED:

                    ALBERT (DEFENSIVE)
        Did I say it was my first time?

                    VIVIAN
        You did. You agree it wasn't?

                    ALBERT
        Sure. What's the big deal?

                    VIVIAN
        You said it was your first time,
        when it was more like a regular
        thing for you. And you weren't
        finding a Bob Dylan still. You were
        planting photos of yourself in the
        archive. Why would you do that?

ALBERT SHIFTS UNCOMFORTABLY.

                    VIVIAN (CONT'D)
        To be noticed? Maybe urgently?

                    ALBERT
        Maybe.

                    VIVIAN
        How did that affect things with
        Brad at the Coalition?

                    ALBERT (DEFENSIVE)
        I wanted my poems to go out with
        the fund-raiser mailing, Brad
        didn't. It was all about Shania and
        Derek Jeter.

                    BERNARD
        So you planted them at
        Schottinger's.

Albert nods, guilty.

                    BERNARD (CONT'D)
        Brad doesn't respect you.

                    ALBERT
        No, he doesn't.

                    BERNARD
        Yet you brought him into the Open
        Spaces Coalition. Why?

CONTINUED: (2)

>   ALBERT
>   To get a corporate sponsor and take
>   the cause to another level, why
>   else would I do it?
>
>   BERNARD
>   Like we said, to be noticed.
>
>   ALBERT (REACHING FOR FOLDER)
>   This is absurd. Show me the folder.
>
>   VIVIAN (SNATCHING IT BACK)
>   No! That is not productive.
>
>   BERNARD (HOLDS UP LANGE PHOTO)
>   At the photo archive, you spent a
>   lot of time looking at old Jessica
>   Lange bathing-suit stills.
>
>   ALBERT
>   Only because Lange comes right
>   before Markovski, L-M, when I went
>   to put my photos in there she is, L-
>   M, see?
>
>   BERNARD
>   Albert, baby. Come on.
>
>   ALBERT
>   Is it a crime to look at Lange?
>
>   VIVIAN
>   Have you ever been in love?
>
>   ALBERT
>   What kind of question is that?
>
>   VIVIAN
>   Do you even believe in love?
>
>   BERNARD
>   Or do you only have fantasy
>   relationships because anything else
>   would be too painful?

BERNARD ROLLS THE COCOON TABLE OVER.

>   VIVIAN
>   Excuse me, Bernard, I am making
>   some progress here.

CONTINUED: (3)

                    BERNARD
          So am I, darling, so am I.

HE KISSES VIVIAN AND SHE LEAVES.

                    ALBERT (LOOKING AT COCOON)
          Don't make me do this, it's all
          hating faces I have to chop up with
          machetes.

                    BERNARD
          And then they multiply. We're going
          to address that right now. You
          can't retreat. I'm in your corner.

He pats Albert on the back.

INT. ALBERT'S MIND

The only sound is Albert's breathing: Albert's body
disintegrates to an empty space of grey/blue/gold, with
Albert fading in and out.

                    BERNARD (V.O.)
          OK, Albert, I want you to melt your
          usual identity like you did before.

A JESSICA LANGE GLOSSY FLOATS BY. THEN DAWN CAMPBELL COMES
INTO VIEW UNDOING HER SHIRT.

                    DAWN
          Stop looking at me. I said stop
          looking at me.

ANOTHER RESTAURANT FLASHBACK:

                    BRAD
          Dawn is going to love doing spots
          for your cause.

                    ALBERT
          Who's Dawn?

                    BRAD
          Miss Huckabees, Dawn. She loves
          your poems -- that one about the
          rock.

                    ALBERT
          Nobody sits like this rock sits --

(CONTINUED)

CONTINUED:

                    BRAD
          That's the one. She also loves
          forests and meadows, she loves
          getting outside, we'll throw the
          jet skis on the trailer, head up to
          the mountains --

                    ALBERT
          Wait a second, you go out with Miss
          Huckabees?

                    BRAD
          She was doing some print work for
          us, wanted to do TV spots, so we
          met here, and she's wearing --

                    BERNARD (V.O.)
          Albert, where are you? Come on,
          don't leave me.

A PICTURE OF DAWN AND BRAD FLOATS BY.

                    BERNARD (V.O.) (CONT'D)
          Picture a tree in a field. Come
          on, let me guide you.

A TREE APPEARS IN AN ABSTRACT LAVENDER BACKGROUND.

                    BERNARD (CONT'D)
          Now put someone you respect up in
          the tree.

Albert appears with Brad sitting above him in a tree.

                    BRAD (IN TREE)
          Dickweed.

                    ALBERT
          Still Brad Stand.

                    BERNARD
          Let him be there. Add someone else.

                    ALBERT
          Like who?

                    BERNARD
          Someone who understands things, who
          can help you.

                                        (CONTINUED)

CONTINUED: (2)

> ALBERT (O.S.)
> Who do you use?

BERNARD POINTS TO A FRAMED PHOTO OF MAGRITTE ON THE WALL.

> BERNARD
> I use Magritte, the Belgian
> surrealist.

> ALBERT
> I got someone.

> BERNARD
> Who is it?

CUT TO INT. ALBERT'S MIND -

> ALBERT
> Mrs. Schirmir.

MRS. SCHIRMIR, a high-school English teacher in her late 50s, in glasses, sits near Brad in the tree.

> BERNARD (O.S.)
> Who's that?

> ALBERT
> High-school English teacher. She
> helped me.

Brad pushes Mrs. Schirmer out of the tree.

> ALBERT (CONT'D)
> Oops, there she goes. He knocked
> her out of the tree.

> BERNARD (O.S.)
> Mrs. Schirmer has a vacuum cleaner
> that sucks up fear.

A HOOVER VACUUM APPEARS IN MRS. SCHIRMER'S HANDS. DARK STREAMS ARE SUCKED OUT OF ALBERT INTO MRS. SCHIRMER'S vacuum.

> BERNARD (CONT'D)
> Now she sends you rays of security
> and complete acceptance. You don't
> have to do anything. You feel
> totally loved and safe, it's a done
> deal.

Gold orange rays from Mrs. Schirmer envelop Albert in a glow, TILL BRAD CHOPS HER HEAD OFF WITH A MACHETE.

CONTINUED:

                    ALBERT
          He chopped her head off.

                    BERNARD (O.S.)
          She's back in the tree. She's
          indestructible.

Mrs. Schirmer reappears; Brad takes her vacuum and sucks her
into it. Albert frantically swings a machete, chopping up
Brad in a rage.

                    ALBERT (CHOPPING UP BRAD)
          RAHHHHHH.

                    BERNARD
          Hold on --

INT. BERNARD'S OFFICE

Bernard unzips the Gortex suit. Albert is out breath.

                    BERNARD
          You're doing well. Don't give up.
          Didn't she vacuum a lot?

                    ALBERT (SWEATY)
          But then he vacuumed her, and then
          I chopped him up. Man.

                    BERNARD
          Albert, I'm going to let you in on
          a couple of secrets: First, your
          mind is always focused on
          something, so it may as well be
          something helpful like Mrs.
          Schirmir and her vacuum. Second,
          there is no you and me.

                    ALBERT
          So there's just... nothing.

                    BERNARD
          Third, there's no such thing as
          nothing. There's the blanket.
          Remember?

                    ALBERT
          I thought I understood the blanket,
          but now I'm not sure.

                                        CUT TO:

HUCKABEES FLAGS AND BAGS COMMERCIAL WITH DAWN.

>   DAWN
>   "Flags and Bags. Huckabees says
>   Happy Birthday, Mr. President.
>   Fifty percent off all knapsacks and
>   pocketbooks. Oh say, can you see
>   how good this looks? Let freedom
>   ring! At Huckabees, the Everything
>   Store."

INT. VIVIAN'S OFFICE - DAY

BRAD STAND SITS IN A CHAIR FACING BERNARD, READING A POEM
INTO A SMALL VIDEO CAMERA.

>   BRAD (READS)
>   "Huckabees, cornucopia of stuff we
>   all want, but what happened to the
>   gazelles, were they squashed under
>   the CD department?" How ya doin',
>   Albert?

Albert is shocked as he walks into the room with Vivian.

>   ALBERT
>   What are you doing here, Brad?

>   VIVIAN
>   I met Brad when I was investigating
>   you. He called with his own
>   existential conundrum.

>   BRAD
>   I'm really glad I found out about
>   these people.

>   ALBERT (AGITATED)
>   That's bullshit, he doesn't care
>   about things like this. Where's the
>   African guy, I want to see the
>   African guy.

>   BRAD
>   Dude, what are you talking about?

CONTINUED:

                    ALBERT (AGITATED)
          And why is he writing poetry? There
          are no goddamn gazelles in North
          America, Brad, and buildings
          squashing nature, that's MY
          imagery, not yours. You don't even
          write poems.

                    BERNARD
          Everyone's in-take procedure is
          different, Albert. I asked Brad to
          write a poem.

                    ALBERT
          I already won, we're the same,
          Brad, it's all the blanket so --
          (in a method trance) I can use Mrs.
          Schirmer.

He SUDDENLY stares in a trance at the floor.

                    BERNARD
          There you go, give it a shot.

Vivian, Bernard, Brad watch as Albert closes his eyes.

                    ALBERT (EYES CLOSED, CALMER)
          How are things at the Coalition,
          Brad?

                    BRAD (WARM)
          Great. Much smoother.

                    ALBERT (EYES CLOSED)
          I'm hoping to come back, that we'll
          work things out.

                    BRAD
          I don't think that's gonna happen,
          my friend.

                    ALBERT (EYES CLOSED)
          I'm still in the charter, I built
          the Coalition from scratch.

                    BRAD
          Well, I don't mean to cramp you
          here.

                    ALBERT (OPENS EYES, ANGRY)
          THAT'S WHAT YOU MEAN TO DO. THAT'S
          EXACTLY WHAT YOU MEAN TO DO.

(CONTINUED)

CONTINUED: (2)

                    BRAD
          What?

                    ALBERT (MIMICS)
          What?

                    BRAD
          What?

                    ALBERT
          What? Do you see what he's doing?
          Tell them what you're doing.

                    BRAD
          Whoa, what?

                    ALBERT
          God, he's come here to conquer you
          just like he's conquered my
          Coalition. And now he is here,
          today, to unnerve me so that when
          Orrin comes to town I'll blow it.
          That's what you mean to do. Tell
          them that's what you mean to do.

                    BRAD
          Albert, please.

                    ALBERT
          Oh my God, Brad, you're killing me.

                    BRAD
          What are you talking about?

                    ALBERT
          What am I talking about? OK, when
          Orrin comes I'll blow it and I'll
          get kicked out of the charter and
          then he can do whatever he wants
          with the Coalition.

                    VIVIAN
          Who's Orrin?

                    ALBERT
          The Open Spaces National Director.
          He's coming to review our charter.

                    BRAD
          I hope this isn't about Dawn. He
          has a crush on my girlfriend.

(CONTINUED)

CONTINUED: (3)

                    ALBERT
That's crazy.

                    BRAD
Then why do you stare at her?

                    ALBERT
She's a model.

                BRAD (TAUNTING)
AHHHH --

                    ALBERT
I'm going home.

                    VIVIAN
Stay for Mancala Hour, Albert.

                    ALBERT
Yeah, I'm gonna have a fucking ball
at Mancala Hour.

                    VIVIAN
Maybe he should meet his Other.

           BERNARD (SUDDENLY UNCOMFORTABLE)
What, Tommy? No, that's a bad idea
right now.

                    VIVIAN
A dicey move, but potentially
inspired. Give them both a
connection.

                    BERNARD
He's in a bad direction, it could
spread to Albert.

                    VIVIAN
You said Tommy was gonna be fine,
what did you leave out?

           BERNARD (PECKS HER AND LEAVES)
Nothing. OK, give him his Other.

                    VIVIAN
The connection will come back to
us, Bernard, it all comes around
like you say. Take the long view.

VIVIAN'S OFFICE - CONTINUOUS

(CONTINUED)

CONTINUED: (4)

                        ALBERT
              What's the Other?

                        VIVIAN
              Shhhh.

Vivian leads Albert into ANOTHER OFFICE.

INT. ANOTHER OFFICE - CONTINUOUS

MRS. ECHEVARRIA, 80-year-old toothless Andalusian widow in
black with a scarf on her head, sits impassively with her
TRANSLATOR, a man of about 50 in glasses, tie, sweater.
Albert points to Mrs. Echevarria. TOMMY CORN is there.

MRS. ECHEVARRIA (SINGS)	TRANSLATOR
En los anos treinta, viviamos sin agua, no habia comida, ni aceitunas, ni alma de vida. Ay, ni conejo en el horno! Combinabamos saltamontes y haciamos pan.	In the 30s, there was drought. There was no crop, no olives, no soul of life. Oh, no rabbit in the oven! We mashed the locusts and made bread.

TOMMY CORN	TRANSLATOR
I don't get it. Are you going to talk about petroleum or not?	No lo comprendo. Vas ha hablar del petroleo o no?

                        TRANSLATOR
              You have received your answer.

                        TOMMY CORN
              Because the petroleum situation
              wasn't created by nature like the
              drought, or the olives or any of
              that, it was created by people who
              act like nothing's happening when
              it's causing all the problems.

                        VIVIAN
              Only one question, Tommy. Uno.

                        TOMMY CORN
              OK, here's the question --

                        VIVIAN
              I think you already had your
              question and your answer.

CONTINUED:

                    TOMMY CORN
          OK, forget petroleum. Why is it
          that people only ask themselves
          deep questions when something
          really bad happens, and then they
          forget all about it later, and how
          come people are self-destructive,
          and third, I refuse to use
          petroleum, and there's no way I can
          stop its use in my lifetime, is
          there? I mean Jimmy Carter would
          have a great electric car by now. I
          could have a Cadillac Escalade and
          it would be electric. I wouldn't
          have to ride my bicycle.

                    VIVIAN
          That's three questions.

                    TOMMY CORN
          I paid my money, and I want
          answers.

                    VIVIAN
          Mrs. Echevarria visits us once a
          year. She's sort of a little treat
          for our clients. Her time's
          limited. She needs to leave soon to
          see a client in Sun Valley.

Mrs. Echevarria chews her gums.

                    VIVIAN (CONT'D)
          Tommy, we wanted you to meet
          Albert.

                    TOMMY CORN
          I thought you said next week.

                    VIVIAN
          Turns out he can use the connection
          sooner than later. Tommy's been
          working with us since September 11.
          He'll be your Other.

Tommy shakes Albert's hand.

                    ALBERT
          Is this like a, what is it exactly?

                    TOMMY CORN
          A buddy system, I think.

CONTINUED: (2)

                    VIVIAN
          When we dismantle, it can get
          pretty rough so it helps to have a
          friend going through the same.

Albert and Tommy stare at each other almost tenderly.

                    TOMMY CORN
          You drive a car?

                    ALBERT
          A bike. Sometimes I take the bus.

                    TOMMY CORN
          Good. That's good. I like it. I can
          see why they put us together. Tommy
          Corn.

Tommy reaches over shaking Albert's hand.

                    ALBERT
          Albert Markovski.

                    TOMMY CORN
          I'll be your Other.

                    VIVIAN
          Yes, wonderful, now please join us
          for Mancala Hour.

INT. RECEPTION AREA - CONTINUOUS

An old Latin jazz album plays. Bernard takes Vivian into his
arms for a dance among others dancing. Albert and Tommy sit
and play mancala, a board game with moveable stones.

                    TOMMY CORN
          What's happening with your case?

                    ALBERT
          I wish I knew. They won't let me
          see my coincidence file.

                    TOMMY CORN
          You want them to solve a
          coincidence? That's why you came
          here?

                    ALBERT
          Yeah.

He stares at DAWN, dancing with Bobby across the room.

                                        (CONTINUED)

CONTINUED:

                    TOMMY CORN
          Who's the girl?

                    ALBERT
          The Voice of Huckabees.

                    TOMMY CORN
          "Tops and mops."

                    ALBERT
          Right.

                    TOMMY CORN
          I doubt your coincidence is
          meaningful.

                    ALBERT
          Why?

                    TOMMY CORN
          I have a book by a French thinker
          named Caterine Vauban --

                    BERNARD (DANCING BY)
          That book is deeply flawed, Tommy.

Bernard and Vivian dance off to the other side of the room.

                    TOMMY CORN
          She says the same thing they say
          here about dismantling your day-to-
          day reality to see the big picture.

                    ALBERT
          Then what's the difference?

                    TOMMY CORN
          Here they say everything's
          connected in the blanket. But
          Vauban says nothing's connected.
          It's random and cruel, so it
          doesn't matter what you do.

                    BERNARD (DANCING BY)
          That's nihilism, Tommy.

                    TOMMY CORN
          They find it a little threatening,
          but it's very convincing.
                    (MORE)

CONTINUED: (2)

           TOMMY CORN (CONT'D)
My ex won't let me see my daughter
and she's brainwashing her to not
think or feel. What kind of reality
is that?

           ALBERT (POINTS TO DETECTIVES)
Not this one.

           TOMMY CORN
I think you should just look at
your file if you want to.

           ALBERT
How am I gonna do that?

           TOMMY CORN
I'll distract them, you slip in for
the file. Here comes your boy, act
natural.

           BRAD (WALKS UP)
Are you playing mancala?

           ALBERT
I didn't know you were interested
in existential questions, Brad.

           BRAD
Why? 'Cause I'm a dumb sales
executive instead of a sensitive
artist like you?

           ALBERT
I never heard you talk about it,
that's all.

           BRAD
Why do you think I joined the Open
Spaces Coalition?

           ALBERT
I thought you cared about the
issue, but you obviously had
another agenda.

           BRAD
I read Phil Jackson's "Sacred
Hoops" when Huckabees got the
galleys, and I didn't read it for
work, I read it because I have
plenty of questions.

(CONTINUED)

CONTINUED: (3)

> ALBERT
> Aren't they mostly sports questions
> in that book?

> BRAD (ANGRY, TRYING TO BE NICE)
> No. Come on, man. Phil Jackson's a
> thinker. He's a smart guy.

> ALBERT
> That was an honest question.

> TOMMY CORN
> It felt a little hostile, but I
> feel the same thing from him.

> BRAD
> Who the hell are you?

> TOMMY CORN
> Who the hell are you?

TOMMY TIPS THE TABLE, SCATTERING THE MANCALA PIECES ALL OVER
THE FLOOR, BRAD STEPS BACK, TOMMY GRABS DAWN TO DANCE. ALBERT
SLIPS AWAY.

> BRAD (PUTS A HAND ON TOMMY'S ARM)
> Don't be an idiot.

TOMMY pushes Brad, who falls onto other clients.

> BOY (LAUGHING COMPULSIVELY)
> That's so funny he pushed him!

> TURKISH MAN
> Eet ees not funny.

> BOY'S MOTHER
> He laughs when he's scared.

> BERNARD (HELPING BRAD)
> Are you all right?

INT. VIVIAN'S OFFICE - CONTINUOUS

Albert sneaks into Vivian's office and rifles through
Vivian's files.

INT. RECEPTION - CONTINUOUS

Bernard and Vivian talking simultaneously to Brad and Tommy.

INT. VIVIAN'S OFFICE - CONTINUOUS

ALBERT FINDS HIS FILE, OPENS IT. Sees a PHOTO OF THE AFRICAN
MAN in a doorman uniform, captioned "STEVEN Nimieri, SUDANESE
REFUGEE, DOORMAN; LIVES AT 155 TRACY ST." Albert frantically
writes this down. THE DOOR OPENS, BOBBY THE RECEPTIONIST
WALKS IN.

> BOBBY
> What are you doing?

> ALBERT
> Bernard, and the poetry thing, but
> it's OK now 'cause I got it.

He walks past him and out.

INT. RECEPTION AREA - CONTINUOUS

Albert walks back in to find Bernard standing between Tommy
and Brad, a hand on each of their chests.

> BERNARD
> In infinity, it's a loop where
> you've had every relationship
> possible: brothers, mother and son,
> husband and wife, predator and --

> BOBBY
> SECURITY BREACH! HE BROKE INTO HIS
> FILE.

Everyone gasps.

> VIVIAN
> What did you do, Albert?

> ALBERT
> It's my investigation now?

> BERNARD
> Albert, you think you know what
> you're doing but you haven't even
> begun to dismantle your identity or
> your fear.

> TOMMY CORN
> Albert's gotta do what he's gotta
> do. (to Dawn) Sorry I grabbed you.

Albert and Tommy walk out.

EXT. SUBURBAN STREETS - DAY

Albert and Tommy ride their bikes.

EXT. TRACY ST. - DAY

Albert and Tommy see MR. NIMIERI THE DOORMAN from afar. He
wears his DOORMAN'S UNIFORM watching kids play basketball in
the driveway of a suburban ranch house.

>   MR. NIMIERI
>   Hello, it is you, my goodness.

>   ALBERT
>   Yes, it is me. Albert. This is my
>   friend, Tommy.

>   MR. NIMIERI
>   Steven Nimieri.

They shake hands.

>   MR. NIMIERI (CONT'D)
>   Is this yet a fourth coincidence?

>   ALBERT
>   No, I came here on purpose. I've
>   been wondering about our
>   coincidences, what they mean.

>   TOMMY CORN
>   Maybe we could spend some time with
>   you to try to understand it.

>   MR. NIMIERI
>   Perhaps you can be my guests for
>   dinner.

>   TOMMY CORN
>   That would be great.

>   MR. NIMIERI
>   I must ask my mom, wait here.

Tommy joins the kids in basketball.

INT. MR. NIMIERI'S S HOME - DINING TABLE - NIGHT

MR. AND MRS. HOOTEN and their teen children CRICKET and BRET,
plus Mr. Nimieri, Albert, and Tommy hold hands at dinner.

(CONTINUED)

CONTINUED:

                  CRICKET
-- for thine is the kingdom, the
power, and the glory forever and
ever, amen.

Cut to everyone eating. Tommy glances at Albert.

                  ALBERT
How did you end up working as a
doorman, Steven?

                MR. NIMIERI
It is part of our immigration
agreement. We must work.

                MRS. HOOTEN
The building supervisor who hired
Steven is a member of our
congregation.

                   BRET
He was so skinny when he moved in.

           CRICKET (MURMURS CRYPTICALLY)
Skeleton Man from Africaaaa.

Bret and Cricket giggle uncontrollably, Bret spits milk.

                MRS. HOOTEN
What did we say about that?

                MR. HOOTEN
I don't want to hear it again, or
there will be no Internet tonight.

                   BRET
He didn't know what a can opener
was. He opened cans with a big
knife, like at the refugee camp.

                MR. HOOTEN
Patience, Bret.

                 CRICKET
And there aren't lions roaming
around here, but there were in
Sudan and the orphan boys got
chased, and a big alligator bit his
friend's head off. He saw it.

(CONTINUED)

CONTINUED: (2)

                         BRET
              Crocodile. There are no alligators
              in Africa.

                         CRICKET
              He wanted to know where all the
              meat comes from since he doesn't
              see any cows around here.

                         MR. HOOTEN
              That's enough, guys, Steven doesn't
              like to talk about that stuff.

Tommy looks at Steven with empathy.

                         MRS. HOOTEN
              What brought you to the
              philosophical club, Albert?

                         ALBERT
              You mean the existential
              detectives?

                         MR. HOOTEN
              Sounds like a support group.

                         CRICKET
              Why can't he use the church?

                         MRS. HOOTEN
              Sometimes people have additional
              questions to explore.

                         CRICKET
              Like what?

                         ALBERT
              Well, for instance, if the forms of
              this world die, which is more real,
              the me that dies or the me that's
              infinite? Can I trust my habitual
              mind or should I try to look
              beneath those things?

                         MR. HOOTEN (CHUCKLES)
              Sounds like we got a philosopher.

                         CRICKET
              We don't have to ask those
              questions, do we, Mom?

                    MRS. HOOTEN
          No, honey.

                    MR. HOOTEN
          Ya know what happened to the cat,
          Albert?

                    ALBERT (TAKEN ABACK)
          How do you know about my cat?

                    MR. HOOTEN (WINKS)
          The cat got killed by curiosity.

                    ALBERT
          Oh, that cat.

                    BRET
          Do you have a job?

                    MRS. HOOTEN
          Yes, Albert, tell us what you do.

                    ALBERT
          I'm director of the Open Spaces
          Coalition. We fight suburban
          sprawl.

                    CRICKET
          What's suburban sprawl?

                    MR. HOOTEN
          Ask Steven if they could use a
          little suburban sprawl in Sudan.

                    MR. NIMIERI
          Excuse me, Dad?

                    MR. HOOTEN
          Industry, houses, jobs,
          restaurants, food, medicine --

                    ALBERT
          You can still preserve a lot of --

                    MR. HOOTEN
          I beg your pardon, Albert, I wasn't
          finished.

                    ALBERT
          Oh. I'm sorry, go ahead.

CONTINUED: (4)

MR. HOOTEN
Clothes, videos, toys,
cheeseburgers, cars, computer
games, a functioning economy.

ALBERT
You can have a functioning economy
and preserve a lot of open spaces,
with a little planning.

MRS. HOOTEN
Socialism, a complete disaster.

ALBERT (GROWING HEATED)
Then I guess Theodore
Roosevelt was a socialist,
and William Butler Yeats, and
Elizabeth Bishop and Robinson
Jeffers and Henry David
Thoreau and the National
Geographic Society --

CRICKET (WHISPERS)
Skeleton man from Africaaaa.

MR. HOOTEN
You're talking about socialism.

ALBERT (GETTING MORE HEATED)
I'm talking about not covering
every square inch of populated
America with strip malls and houses
till people can't even remember
what happens when you stand alone
in a meadow at dusk.

BRET
What happens in the meadow at dusk?

ALBERT
Everything. Everything.

MRS. HOOTEN
Nothing. Nothing.

TOMMY CORN
It's beautiful.

MR. HOOTEN (MAD)
I happen to work for an electrical
engineering firm, son, and we do a
great deal of commercial and
residential contracts, so if
development stops, so does my pay
check, and then Steven couldn't be
here as our guest, could he? Your
ideas are hurting Steven, Albert.

CONTINUED: (5)

                    ALBERT (HEATED)
I am not hurting Steven. That's an
outrageous accusation.

                 MR. HOOTEN (VERY MAD)
Don't use that tone in my house.

                       ALBERT
I think you started that tone, sir,
and it's entirely possible for your
engineering firm to have all kinds
of contracts and still --

Albert suddenly stares at the table. He closes his eyes as
everyone looks.

                      CRICKET
Why's he closing his eyes?

                   MRS. HOOTEN
Cricket.

                    MR. HOOTEN
Do you have a job, Tommy?

                   TOMMY CORN
I'm a fireman.

                   MRS. HOOTEN
You're a hero, God bless you.

                   TOMMY CORN
I'm no hero. We'd all be heroes if
we'd quit using petroleum.

                    MR. HOOTEN
Excuse me?

                   TOMMY CORN
You say you're Christians living by
Jesus' principles, but are you?

                       BRET
Of course we are.

                      CRICKET
Jesus is never mad at us if we live
with him in our hearts.

                   TOMMY CORN
Well, I hate to break it to you,
but he is, he most definitely is.

CONTINUED: (6)

>   MRS. HOOTEN
>   Steven, you've brought blasphemous
>   socialists into our house.

>   MR. NIMIERI
>   I'm sorry, Dad, I did not know.

>   MR. HOOTEN
>   Steve-O. I'm disappointed.

Steven looks down, ashamed.

>   MRS. HOOTEN
>   Now look, he's sad.

>   MR. HOOTEN
>   I'm sorry, Steve-O. My bad, you
>   didn't know.

>   TOMMY CORN
>   You should be ashamed of yourself.

>   MR. HOOTEN
>   I should be what?

>   TOMMY CORN
>   You should be ashamed of yourself.

>   MR. HOOTEN
>   And why is that? Why should I be
>   ashamed of myself?

>   TOMMY CORN   MR. HOOTEN
>   You're a hypocrite. You're   I'm a what? How is that?
>   misleading these children.

>   TOMMY CORN
>   'Cause you're the destroyer man.

>   MR. HOOTEN
>   How am I the destroyer?

>   TOMMY CORN
>   I saw that SUV out there.

>   MR. HOOTEN
>   Oh, my car's the destroyer. You
>   want to know how many miles per
>   gallon I get?

DIALOGUE CONTINUES OFF SCREEN. CUT TO:

CONTINUED: (7)

                ALBERT
Steven, I really need to ask you a
question. It's why I came here.
Why are autographs so important to
you?

                MR. NIMIERI
It is a pastime of this family
which they have taught to me and
which I can now carry on.

                MRS. HOOTEN (O.S.)
It's just for fun, it's for
entertainment. No games at the
table, please.

                BRET (PLAYING COMPUTER GAME)
YESSS, 260, I reached Omega Level.

                MR. NIMIERI (SADLY)
I cannot achieve Omega level.

                MR. HOOTEN
GOD GAVE US OIL! HE GAVE IT TO US!

                TOMMY CORN
HE GAVE YOU A BRAIN, TOO.

                MR. HOOTEN (TO ALBERT)
I want you sons of bitches out now.

                TOMMY CORN
If Hitler were alive, he'd tell us
NOT to think about oil.

                MRS. HOOTEN (CRYING)
YOU'RE THE HITLER. I GAVE A
SUDANESE REFUGEE A HOME.

                TOMMY CORN
How did Sudan happen? Could it be
related to dictatorships we support
for some stupid reason?

                MR. HOOTEN
YOU SHUT UP, YOU GET OUT.

                TOMMY CORN
You shut up.

Tommy and Albert head to the door.

CONTINUED: (8)

                    ALBERT
          See you later, Steve.

                    TOMMY CORN
          God bless you.

EXT. NIMIERI'S SUBURBAN HOME - NIGHT.

The door slams on Albert and Tommy, who stop on the sidewalk
and look at each other like "holy shit."

Vivian and Bernard climb out of the bushes, removing their
headphones.

                    VIVIAN
          You hesitated over the mention of a
          cat. What does that mean?

                    ALBERT
          Nothing. Just like my coincidence.

                    VIVIAN
          The cat seemed to hit a nerve.

                    ALBERT
          Yeah, I once had a cat, you caught
          me. You're amazing.

                    BERNARD
          The method helped. I saw it,
          Albert.

                    TOMMY CORN
          What method? Come on with that
          method. It's a tranquilizer so we
          don't get pissed about the painful,
          ugly truth.

                    BERNARD
          No, it penetrates the unified
          infinity of everything.

                    ALBERT (UNLOCKING HIS BIKE)
          We're not in infinity, we're in the
          suburbs.

Albert and Tommy TAKE OFF ON THEIR BIKES.

EXT. SUBURBAN STREET - CONTINUOUS

Bernard and Vivian jog alongside Albert and Tommy as they
ride their bikes.

CONTINUED:

>   BERNARD
>   Infinity's everywhere, that's what
>   makes it infinity.

>   TOMMY CORN (RIDING BIKE)
>   Mr. Nimieri's an orphan who was
>   chased by soldiers and crocodiles.
>   Where does your love glow fit in?

>   BERNARD (LEANING OUT CAR WINDOW)
>   It's connected, Albert and Mr.
>   Nimieri share a great deal, we just
>   don't know if -- OH MY GOD!

A LIGHT YELLOW TOWN CAR PULLS UP ON THE OTHER SIDE OF ALBERT
AND TOMMY AS THEY RIDE. CATERINE STARES AS SHE DRIVES.

>   VIVIAN (TERRIFIED)(O.S.)
>   What is she doing here?

>   BERNARD (O.S.)
>   It's Caterine!

Vivian and Bernard stop running as Caterine, Tommy and Albert
keep going.

>   VIVIAN (VERY UPSET)
>   This is much worse that we thought.

>   BERNARD
>   Yeah. A lot worse.

ALBERT STARES AT CATERINE FOR A MOMENT, THEN ALBERT AND TOMMY
TURN A CORNER ON THEIR BIKES.

>   TOMMY CORN
>   Come on!

>   ALBERT
>   The meeting's going down right now,
>   let's go.

Tommy and Albert speed off.

INT. HUCKABEES CORPORATE - CONFERENCE ROOM - DAY

Albert stands addressing the Coalition Members as ORRIN
SPENCE, 40, Director of The National Open Spaces Coalition,
tries to calm everyone down. Tommy Corn is there.
Construction Worker #3 is there. The Frosh Girls wear their
Shania Open Spaces T-shirts.

CONTINUED:

                    ORRIN SPENCE
          Hey everybody, calm down! The
          National Office recognizes the
          charter. We want to give the
          director a chance to even the keel
          today.

                    ALBERT
          Thank you, Orrin. First of all, I
          want to apologize for my part of
          the fight that I had with Brad
          Stand a little while ago over the
          poems that did not go out with the
          Shania mailing.

                    ANGELA
          Where's Brad?

All the ladies in the room chime in.

                    TOMMY CORN
          It's all Brad, Brad, Brad.

                    ALBERT
          So the big benefit's happening
          really soon. I know Brad's running
          it and it's going to go really
          great, but we're overlooking our
          core issues --

                    DARLENE
          Brad is not here.

                    ALBERT
          -- and to get us back on track, I
          have a new poem I'd like to read.

                    ANGELA FRANCO
          Point of order. I want to discuss
          this strategy of poems.

                    TOMMY CORN
          Excuse me, ma'am. Poems are
          amazing, they help you in your mind
          transform --

                    ANGELA FRANCO
          Who the hell are you?

CONTINUED: (2)

> TOMMY CORN
> I'm with Albert. They will help you
> to transform your mind into
> thinking differently. You guys
> need this, OK? This is great.

> ALBERT (READS HIS POEM)
> This is called "An Open Meadow":
> "An open meadow, an open marsh, a
> crane flying in a cloudless sky --"

Brad walks in with a life-size cut-out of SHANIA TWAIN.

> ANGELA FRANCO
> Brad's here!

> BRAD (CHEERFUL)
> What's happening guys?

> MARY JANE HUTCHINSON
> Is that for my grandson?

> BRAD
> Indeed it is, Mary Jane.

> MARY JANE HUTCHINSON
> You are a dear, dear man.

Brad hands the Shania cut-out across Albert toward Mary Jane.

> ALBERT
> Hold on, please.

> BRAD
> You got it, sweetheart?

Albert tries to help and accidentally rips off Shania's head.

> MARY JANE HUTCHINSON
> Oh, no.

> BRAD
> Good job Albert.

> MARY JANE HUTCHINSON
> Can it be taped?

> ALBERT
> Excuse me! If I could just finish
> reading this poem, we'll review the
> strategy, OK?
> (MORE)

CONTINUED: (3)

                    ALBERT (CONT'D)
          "The cranes flying above in a
          cloudless sky, and not a McDonald's
          in sight" --

                    BRAD
          Relax, we're not doing the poems.

                    ALBERT
          Don't give me the "relax" thing.

                    TOMMY CORN
          Let him read the poem.

                    ANGELA FRANCO (POINTS AT TOMMY)
          That man is not a member of the
          Coalition.

                    ALBERT
          He's a local fireman, we want him
          on our side. Besides, who are those
          guys? (He points to the Dexicorp
          guys) They're not members.

                    BRAD
          They're working on the benefit,
          don't be so negative.

                    ANGELA FRANCO
          I move to empower Brad Stand to act
          on behalf of the Coalition --

                    ALBERT
          POINT OF ORDER.

                    BRAD (TO ALBERT)
          Use the method. Conflict is an
          illusion.

                    ALBERT
          Shut up, Brad.

                    TOMMY CORN
          Yeah, shut up.

                    ORRIN SPENCE
          Albert, that's not how a director
          behaves.

                    TOMMY CORN
          Why are you guys wasting all your
          time fighting each other? Put the
          egos aside for a moment.
                         (MORE)

CONTINUED: (4)

> TOMMY CORN (CONT'D)
> We've got a deadly petroleum
> situation, not to mention cystic
> fibrosis, civil war in Africa, a
> handgun problem, toxic fish.
> You've got children in your own
> community going to prison. Father
> Flavin doesn't have the money to
> help them.

> BRAD
> Father Flavin? Orrin, this is
> exactly the unfocused, idealistic
> approach of Albert Markovski that's
> killing us.   Our mission has
> nothing to do with this nut's
> petroleum fixation --

TOMMY EXPLODES FROM HIS SEAT AND DECKS BRAD WITH ONE PUNCH.

> HARRISON
> RIGHT ON.

> MARY JANE HUTCHINSON
> My Lord in heaven.

She and Darlene, Angela, every woman there, rush to Brad.

> ORRIN SPENCE (TO ALBERT)
> You are OUT of the charter, man.

> ANGELA FRANCO (HELPING BRAD)
> I move to vote.

> MARY JANE HUTCHINSON
> Second.

> ORRIN SPENCE
> All in favor of Brad assuming
> powers to negotiate on behalf of
> the Open Spaces say aye.

> EVERYONE (BUT HARRISON, ALBERT, TOMMY)
> AYE.

> ORRIN SPENCE
> The motion passes.

> BRAD
> Thank you, Orrin. Thank you
> everyone. A new beginning!

APPLAUSE. Tommy puts his arm around crestfallen Albert and
escorts him out.

INT. HALLWAY OF HUCKABEES CORPORATE - CONTINUOUS

Dialogue continues as Tommy leads Albert down the hallway,
trailed by Froshes and Construction Worker #3.

                    TOMMY CORN
          Be strong, because you're going to
          be back. Don't worry about those
          people, they don't appreciate you.

Tommy and Albert stop and huddle together over a railing.

                    TOMMY CORN (CONT'D)
          Albert, what happened there is
          reality. It's cruelty and it's
          chaos. The detectives were wrong.
          What were you trying to do? You
          were trying to do a good thing,
          right? And look what happened.

Albert looks dejected and sad, trying not to cry.

                    TOMMY CORN (CONT'D)
          I'm going to the other side Albert.
          I seriously suggest you consider
          coming with me, as my other.

Vivian and Bernard come out from behind a pillar from across
the atrium.

          BERNARD   VIVIAN
Albert!   Tommy!

Albert, Tommy, et al. begin running away as Bernard and
Vivian follow.

                    TOMMY CORN (CONT'D)
          You're wrong. You're full of shit.
          You guys have got nothing to offer,
          man.

                    BERNARD (SHOUTS TO TOMMY)
          THIS IS A PERFECT OPPORTUNITY TO
          DISMANTLE, DON'T BLOW IT.

                    ALBERT
          Stay away from me!

                    BERNARD (WALKING TOWARD ALBERT)
          Albert! Tommy! Stop! Look! Listen!

                                              (CONTINUED)

CONTINUED:

Albert and Tommy stop to listen.

                    BERNARD (CONT'D)
          Throughout infinity, your energy
          recycles into every possible
          relation to everyone else's energy,
          even Brad's: you've been predator
          and prey with him, friends,
          enemies, brothers, sisters, child,
          parent.

Albert closes his eyes.

INT. ALBERT'S MIND --

BRAD HAS A WOMAN'S LONG HAIR AND BREASTS AND HOLDS BABY
ALBERT, WITH ALBERT'S ADULT FACE, TO NURSE HIM.

                    MOTHER/BRAD IN ALBERT'S MIND
          I give and I give and I give and he
          takes and he takes and he takes.

                    ALBERT
          Mama.

                                        CUT BACK TO:

Albert opens his eyes.

                    ALBERT (CONT'D)
          Yuck!

They run from Bernard and Vivian.

                    TOMMY CORN
          It's a romantic fantasy and you
          left that part out when you were
          taking my cash and I want it back.

                    ALBERT
          Yeah, and if I wasn't pro bono I'd
          want my money back, too.

                    TOMMY CORN
          Send it to my ex, to my kid.

INT. LOBBY OF HUCKABEES CORPORATE - CONTINUOUS

Albert runs across the huge, stark glass and white marble
lobby. He grabs his bike from a security desk.

CONTINUED:

                    SECURITY GUARD
      HEY, sign out!

               ALBERT (RUNNING OUT)
      IT'S MY BIKE. Tommy, come on!

                  TOMMY CORN
      Go, I'll block for you!

EXT. HUCKABEES CORPORATE - CONTINUOUS

Albert bolts out of the building. Tommy signs for his bike,
blocks the detectives, then takes off.

Albert runs down Route 4 with his bike, chased by the
detectives and Tommy with his bike.

EXT. ROUTE 4 - CONTINUOUS

Bernard and Vivian stop running, sweaty, out of breath.

EXT. ROUTE 9 - DAY

Albert rides his bike, sweaty, agitated. He stops at a STOP
SIGN.

                    ALBERT
      Cocksucker! Motherfucking bitch ass
      motherfucking cocksucker! You're
      all a big bunch of babies.

CATERINE'S TOWN CAR pulls up alongside. Caterine Vauban looks
at Albert through her closed window. She pulls up in her car.

            ALBERT (TO CATERINE) (CONT'D)
      Maybe I should just quit. I mean
      what's the point of life anyway?

                 CATERINE
      I can answer these questions for
      you.

                    ALBERT
      You can? Because I don't think the
      other guys are doing such a hot
      job.

                 CATERINE
      Believe me, I can.

He looks at her. THE TRUNK POPS OPEN. He puts his bike in the
trunk, and gets in the car. She pulls out.

THEY RIDE IN SILENCE. ALBERT WIPES HIS BROW.

>   ALBERT
>   You're the writer Tommy's into,
>   aren't you?

>   CATERINE VAUBAN
>   Are you unhappy with their work?

>   ALBERT
>   I think I'm ready to cross over to
>   your side.

>   CATERINE VAUBAN
>   Tell me about your case.

>   ALBERT
>   You seem to be following it pretty
>   closely, why don't you tell me?

>   CATERINE VAUBAN
>   You were miserable, obsessed with
>   your strange coincidence...

>   ALBERT
>   Yeah, but they just want to talk
>   about Brad Stand.

They drive past strip malls along Route 4.

>   CATERINE VAUBAN
>   They betrayed you, as he did.

>   ALBERT
>   Yes.

>   CATERINE VAUBAN
>   Betrayal embodies the universal
>   truth you seek.

>   ALBERT
>   What truth?

>   CATERINE VAUBAN
>   Cruelty, manipulation.
>   Meaninglessness.

>   ALBERT
>   Yeah.

(CONTINUED)

CONTINUED:

He looks at her. She turns a corner. The car stops. DOOR
OPENS AND TOMMY SLIDES INTO THE FRONT SEAT, SHOVING ALBERT
CLOSER TO CATERINE.

> CATERINE VAUBAN
> Did they follow you?

> TOMMY CORN
> I lost them on Route 4. I'm glad
> you came, Albert. This is the place
> to be. When you know the universe
> sucks, you've got nothing to lose.
> That gives you (in French) *la
> force.*

> ALBERT
> *La force.* What's that?

> TOMMY CORN
> It's French for strength.

Albert picks up Caterine's book from the dashboard.

> ALBERT
> Is there a method here?

> TOMMY CORN
> You deconstruct your mind into the
> blackness, and accept it for what
> it is: nothing. No glowing guides,
> no infinite mothers or crap like
> that.

CAR STOPS.

> ALBERT
> My coincidence is meaningless,
> isn't it?

> CATERINE
> Think, Albert, have you betrayed
> yourself?

She gets out of the car.

> ALBERT
> HEY, wait a second -- what are we
> doing here? I DON'T WANT TO GO INTO
> THIS BUILDING, STOP.

CONTINUED:

HE LOOKS A BIT PANICKED. ALBERT JUMPS OUT AND RUNS INTO THE
BUILDING AFTER HER, FOLLOWED BY TOMMY.

                    TOMMY CORN (YELLING AFTER ALBERT)
          Trust her, Albert!

INT. LOBBY OF HIGH-RISE BUILDING - DAY

Albert sees Caterine run across the lobby of this residential
building, HAND A NOTE TO Mr. Nimieri, THE DOORMAN AND
DISAPPEAR INTO THE ELEVATOR.

                    ALBERT
          (to Mr. Nimieri) What did she give
          you?

HE PULLS AT THE NOTE in Nimieri's hand, Nimieri PULLS IT
BACK.

                    MR. NIMIERI (BACKS AWAY)
          Stay away from me.

Albert lets go and runs into another elevator.

INT. 43RD FLOOR OF HIGH RISE - DAY

Albert rings the bell to apartment 43H. His mother, an
intense Italian-American, 60, opens the door.

                    MRS. SILVER
          Well, this is a rare occasion.

                    ALBERT (TO HIS MOTHER)
          Where is she?

                    MRS. SILVER
          Who?

                    ALBERT
          Caterine.

                    MRS. SILVER
          Who's Caterine?

                    ALBERT
          The woman who's spying on me.

                    MRS. SILVER
          I don't think that's funny.

                    MR. SILVER
          What's happening?

                                              (CONTINUED)

CONTINUED:

ALBERT'S FATHER, a balding man of 62 wearing a bright madras shirt, walks into the foyer.

> MRS. SILVER
> He's making some joke on me.

> MR. SILVER
> Are you making fun of your mother?

> ALBERT
> No.

Albert walks into the quasi-Eames-style, modern living room.

> MRS. SILVER
> How's your poetry job?

> ALBERT
> I got fired from that.

> MRS. SILVER (SARCASTIC)
> You can't even hold the poetry job.

> MR. SILVER
> Brenda, what the hell did you do?

> MRS. SILVER
> I didn't touch it.

> MR. SILVER
> Bullshit, I had this programmed to
> my favorite stations on a timer --

> MRS. SILVER
> Can I please have time with my son?

> MR. SILVER (FIDDLES WITH STEREO)
> Goddamn it.

> MRS. SILVER
> I wanna show him an article on a
> marketing internship.

> MR. SILVER (TURNING IT ON)
> Have you seen this system, Albert?
> State of the art. We've got
> speakers all through the
> house(sings along with radio) "Ohh-
> oh-oh, Get in the action, feel the
> attraction, color my hair, do what
> I dare, ohh-oh-oh --"

CONTINUED: (2)

SUDDENLY CATERINE APPEARS AND TURNS THE STEREO OFF.

> CATERINE
> It will be easier to talk now.

> MRS. SILVER
> Where did she come from?

> MR. SILVER
> How did she get in?

> MRS. SILVER
> Is she with you?

> ALBERT
> I told you I wasn't making a joke.

> CATERINE VAUBAN
> I would like to discuss some
> curious findings.

> MR. SILVER
> Who is this lady?

SHE HOLDS UP A WEATHERED CHILD'S NOTEBOOK.

> CATERINE VAUBAN (cont'd)
> I have found here in your apartment
> a rather troubling piece of
> evidence. Do you recognize the
> handwriting, Mr. Markovski, pardon
> me, Mr. Silver?

> MR. SILVER
> No.

SHE SHOWS THE JOURNAL TO MRS. SILVER.

> CATERINE VAUBAN
> Could you please read the date for
> me?

> ALBERT
> This is silly, let's go.

> MRS. SILVER
> November 17, 1989. Albert was 9.
> This is his journal.

> CATERINE VAUBAN
> Do you mind reading this out loud?

> MRS. SILVER
> Why?

(CONTINUED)

STILLS

Vivian and Bernard
Jaffe on the move.

Jason Schwartzman as
Albert Markovsky.

Mark Wahlberg as
Tommy Corn. "Why
do people only ask
themselves deep ques-
tions when something
really bad happens?"

Jude Law as Brad
Stand and Naomi
Watts as Dawn
Campbell.

Naomi Watts as Dawn
Campbell at work for
Huckabees.

Isabelle Huppert as
Caterine Vauban, a
cocktail of Zen and
satire and nihilism.

Albert's first meeting
with Bernard and
Vivian Jaffe.

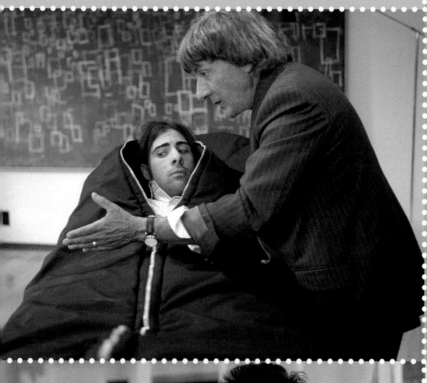

Albert's dismantling
begins.

"Where did you get
this book?"

Vivian Jaffe takes
Albert's case.

The investigation
begins.

D. Russell putting
chalk squares on
Bernard Jaffe's back.

Each other's "other."

Jason and Mark.

"I have a book by a
French thinker named
Caterine Vauban."

"You wanna dance? I love to dance!"

Tommy shoves Brad to create a distraction so Albert can steal his file.

"Albert, what did you do?"

Debating reality outside Mr. Nimieri's house: Is it interconnected and benevolent or chaotic and meaningless?

I thought of this scene as *Casablanca* because people are dancing and drinking but serious matters are being discussed in hushed tones.

On the set.

An Actor Prepares.

He pushed her out of
the tree.

"I have a BMW SUV and I like driving it!"

"You spoke to my fat, sad brother?"

"Shania hates mayonnaise."

Mother and son.

Everyone but Isabelle.

Mr. Hoffman and
Mr. Schwartzman—
Dustin's chair was so
good to sit in.

Jason and Isabelle, Lily and Dustin get ready for a showdown.

Post-coitus.

The second coincidence. Ger Duany is from Sudan and lived the whole nightmare of that exodus.

Goodman, Jude, Mark, Lou and David O. Russell.

Detectives at work
on Brad and Dawn.

"I've thought about
chopping your head
off with a machete
many times, Brad."
"I've thought about
smashing your head
in with a baseball bat,
Albert."

Rehearsing the fight
in the elevator.

Shania!

Isabelle.

David O. Russell and
Jason Schwartzman

Naomi top hat.

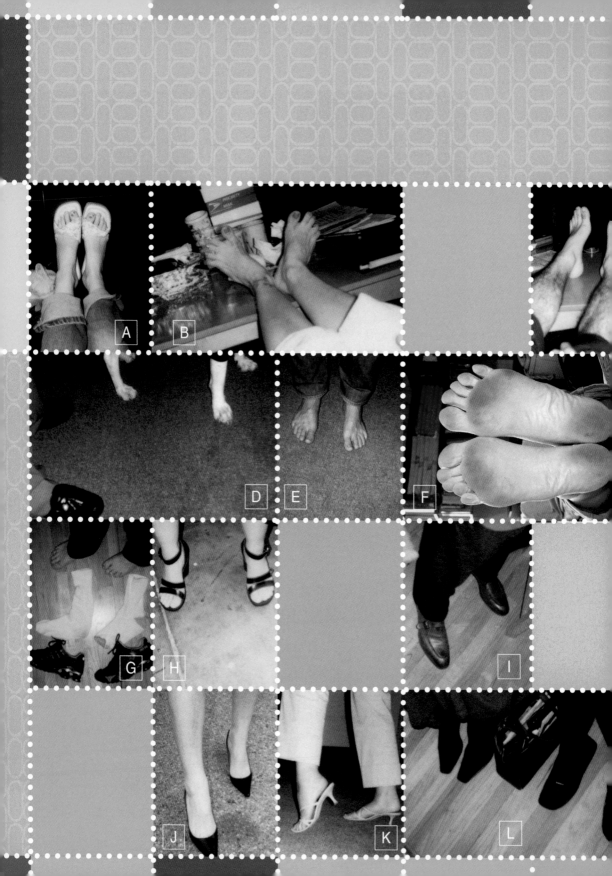

THANK YOU TO THE FOLLOWING:

sla Fisher. B: Ashley. C: Jason Schwartzman. D: Matthew Grillo-Russell & Fred. E: Sacha Baron Cohen.
Bob Thurman. G: Mr. Jonze. H: Shania Twain. I: John Lesher. J. Isabelle Huppert. K: Claudia Lewis.
Breena Camden, Megan Colligan. M: David O. Russell. N: Joe Rudnick. O: Megan Colligan.
Greg Goodman. Q: Naomi Watts. R: Zoe Deschanel. S: Dustin and Lisa Hoffman. T: Tippi Hedren.
Alexander Payne. V: Gia Coppola, Sofia Coppola, and Jason Schwartzman. W: Peter Rice. X: Janet Grillo.

David O. Russell

                    CATERINE
Please.

                    ALBERT
Oh my god.

               MRS. SILVER (READS FROM JOURNAL)
"I came home from school. Mom was
in the kitchen with a strange lady.
Mom told me to go back to my room.
I thought I was in trouble. She
closed my door and said Purree was
hit by a car and killed and then
she took me back to the lady in the
kitchen and asked me to spell words
to show how I was a good speller. I
said I had to go to the bathroom. I
climbed out the window."

Caterine listens intently.

               MRS. SILVER (READS FROM JOURNAL)
                    (CONT'D)
"I went down the block. I see
Barney playing punch ball. He said
I look sad. I told him what
happened to my cat. He said that's
sad, then I cried but I tried not
to, some kids laughed. Barney said
he cried when Rocky died, the kids
stopped laughing." His cat died, it
was sad. What's the point?

                    CATERINE VAUBAN
Nothing strikes you as odd?

                    MR. SILVER
These things happen.

                    ALBERT
See? It's nothing let's go.

                    CATERINE VAUBAN
C'est vrai, the universe is cruel --
But tell me this, Mrs. Silver: The
lady you gave the coffee to --

                    MRS. SILVER
Helen's sister. I can't remember
her name. I only met her once.

                                        (CONTINUED)

CONTINUED: (4)

> CATERINE VAUBAN
> Was there some painful thing about
> this stranger that required your
> immediate attention?

> ALBERT
> I wanna go.

> MRS. SILVER
> No. Helen wasn't home so I offered
> her sister a cup of coffee.

> CATERINE VAUBAN
> Do you agree that Purree meant a
> great deal to Albert?

> MR. SILVER
> You can't make a federal case out
> of the cat.

> CATERINE VAUBAN
> Answer the question, please.

Mr. Silver nervously pours himself a glass of juice.

> MR. SILVER
> I wouldn't know much about the cat,
> I traveled a lot for work.

> ALBERT
> This is embarrassing, I think it's
> unnecessary.

> CATERINE VAUBAN
> Precisely the point.

> MRS. SILVER
> What?

They all look confused, including Albert.

> CATERINE VAUBAN (cont'd)
> You were embarrassed for feeling
> sad about the death of your cat.
> It's painful enough to feel sad,
> but on top of it, to feel
> embarrassed for feeling, that is
> the killer. And then to be asked to
> perform with his spelling ability.
> C'est ca vraiment pire que tout.

(CONTINUED)

                    MRS. SILVER
          How is that my fault? I didn't tell
          him to be embarrassed.

                    CATERINE VAUBAN
          But you did. It was more important
          to have a cup of coffee with a
          perfect stranger than to talk to
          Albert about what, for a small boy,
          is a large tragedy. He climbed out
          the window, a criminal in his own
          house. Why?

                    MRS. SILVER
          I don't know. Why?

                    CATERINE VAUBAN
          I think you do.

                    MRS. SILVER (UPSET)
          No, I don't, stop it.

                    CATERINE VAUBAN
          You do.

                    MR. SILVER
          That's enough, you should go!

                    CATERINE VAUBAN (ANGRY)
          I will not go. Albert has a place
          here, a place you have denied.

                    MRS. SILVER
          This is my house, I can tell him
          what I want.

                    CATERINE VAUBAN
          Yes, your home is a lie.

                    MRS. SILVER
          What does that mean? I gave my
          life to this selfish bastard --

                    CATERINE VAUBAN
          So he could be an ornament to you,
          not a person! (to Mr. Silver)

                    MRS. SILVER
          You bitch! How many kids do have?

Doorbell rings.

CONTINUED: (6)

> CATERINE VAUBAN (GOES TO OPEN DOOR)
> Listen, listen, listen. This is
> your mother.

Mr. Nimieri walks in.

> MR. NIMIERI (HOLDING NOTE)
> You asked me to come up here?

> MRS. SILVER
> What does the doorman have to do
> with this?

> CATERINE VAUBAN
> He was orphaned by civil war, you
> were orphaned by indifference. This
> is one part of your puzzle. Do you
> see?

Mr. Nimieri leaves. The radio comes on again.

> MR. SILVER
> Oh, now the timer's all fucked up,
> Brenda.

ALBERT'S PARENTS CONTINUE TO ARGUE AS HE AND CATERINE WALK
OUT.

DISSOLVE TO INT. ELEVATOR - CONTINUOUS

Caterine takes out a POLAROID CAMERA, OPENS IT, TAKES A PHOTO
OF ALBERT.

INT. LOBBY - CONTINUOUS

The doors open, and Tommy stands in the LOBBY. Tommy nods his
head in understanding as they walk past him, holding hands,
and he follows them out --

EXT. PARENTS BLDG. - DAY

CURBSIDE, CATERINE DRIVES OFF AS ALBERT AND TOMMY WATCH.

> TOMMY
> We'll meet you later at the rock.
> Thanks.

She drives off. Albert and Tommy take a few steps away from
the building and stop.

CONTINUED:

                         ALBERT (UPSET)
               I'm sorry, man, I need like a
               minute to figure this out.

HE STANDS THERE CRYING FOR A MOMENT AS TOMMY WATCHES HIM.

                         TOMMY
               She had to get you to see.

                         ALBERT
               See what?

                         TOMMY
               You were trained to betray yourself
               right here...That's why you
               betrayed yourself by going to Brad.

Albert takes this in. DETECTIVES JOG UP.

                         ALBERT
               Why didn't you figure this out? Why
               didn't you bring me here?

                         VIVIAN
               Because you lied to us. You said
               the African guy was the doorman at
               your friend's building, not your
               parents' building. You encrypted
               the truth. That's how good you are
               at betraying yourself. (now to
               Bernard) I told you we needed facts
               to piece together a theory, that he
               wasn't ready for infinity.

                         TOMMY CORN
               Hey, don't start with that magic
               blanket bullshit, OK?

                         BERNARD
               It's not magic, it's just the way
               things are, Tommy. You and me and
               the air are actually tiny particles
               that are swirling around together.
               Look right here, see?

HE POINTS TO CUBES OFF HIM, ALBERT, TOMMY, VIVIAN --

                         TOMMY (POINTS TO CRACKS)
               What about these SPACES BETWEEN THE
               CUBES, the CRACKS we fall through,
               the holes of nothingness?

                                                    (CONTINUED)

CONTINUED: (2)

                  ALBERT
Exactly, because that's what I just
experienced upstairs.

              BERNARD (POINTS)
LOOK CLOSER, there are tiny
connections linking the larger
cubes.

              TOMMY (POINTS)
And tiny CRACKS between those
connections, more holes to fall
through --

                 BERNARD
But there are even tinier
connections --

                  TOMMY
And even tinier cracks --

                 BERNARD
No, if you zoom in close enough,
you can't find where my nose ends
and space begins, they're unified.

                 ALBERT
So what? I can't see any of this.
Can you see any of this?

                  TOMMY
No, but I wanna debate this
particle cube thing.

                 VIVIAN
You live by what you can't see all
the time, you can't see electric-
ity, can you? You can't see radio
waves, but you accept them.

                 BERNARD
Trust.

                 ALBERT
Fuck trust.

                 BERNARD
You better stay away from Caterine,
Albert, she'll take you down the
path to darkness.

CONTINUED: (3)

                    VIVIAN
          She was our prize graduate student
          until she went astray.

                    ALBERT
          No thanks, I'm gonna stick with the
          cracks and the pain, that's more
          real to me.

                    TOMMY
          WORD.

                    BERNARD
          OK, we're not sweating.

                    VIVIAN
          Yeah, we're gonna work on Brad.

                    BERNARD
          And it's all gonna come back to you
          and interconnection and the cubes.

                    ALBERT
          Are you kidding me? Brad? I'm gonna
          work on that prick, and it's all
          gonna come back to pain and NO
          CONNECTION.

                    TOMMY CORN
          It's on.

Tommy and Albert walk off.

                    VIVIAN
          We'll see.

EXT. BRAD'S BIG SUBURBAN HOUSE - DAY

A large green yard with landscaped shrubs. Vivian peers out
from behind a bush. The sprinkler cuts across her body; she
sneaks across the lawn to another bush, runs across to the
driveway and in her suit leans into a garbage can. Bernard
follows clandestinely behind with listening equipment,
wearing a set of headphones. He crouches near the garbage
cans Vivian rifles.

                    VIVIAN (PULLING OUT GARBAGE)
          Kafka.

She tosses a Kafka book onto the driveway.

CONTINUED:

> VIVIAN (CONT'D)
> He's planting garbage for us.

> BERNARD
> Kafka, that's so fishy.

Bernard shakes his head sadly then --

> BERNARD (WEARING HEADPHONES) (CONT'D)
> Listen to this, she found his poem.

He hands her a second set of headphones; they listen.

INT. BRAD'S HOME KITCHEN - DAY

> BRAD
> Don't do it, don't go in my den.
> I'm not unhappy to be with you
> Dawn.

> DAWN (READS)
> Let me see this. (rips poem out of
> Brad's hands) Quote, "Putting on a
> show, can't say no, inside I'm
> drowning, sighing and frowning."
> That doesn't sound very happy to
> me, does that sound happy to you?

> BRAD
> I only wrote "frowning" because it
> rhymes with "drowning."

> DAWN
> Then why did you need "drowning?"

> BRAD
> To rhyme with "frowning."

> DAWN
> OK. Wait. The first word comes from
> what you want to say, the second
> word has to rhyme -- AND WHY DO
> THEY HAVE TO CREEP AROUND OUR YARD
> AND GO THROUGH THE GARBAGE?

She points out the window at Vivian and Bernard at the
garbage cans; they look at Dawn, WALK TOWARD THE KITCHEN.
VIVIAN AND BERNARD OPEN THE DOOR AND COME IN.

(CONTINUED)

CONTINUED:

                      DAWN (CONT'D)
What is he doing? Stop that. Why is
he sniffing my blouse?

            BERNARD (TOSSES BLOUSE DOWN)
Perspiration indicates stress and
that's kind of high.

Bernard rifles through drawers.

                     VIVIAN
Brad signed a rather comprehensive
contract for unfettered access to
your home --

                     DAWN
It's my home, too, and I didn't
sign anything.

                     VIVIAN
You'll have to work that out with
Brad. The mortgage is in his name
and you're not married.

                 DAWN (CHAGRINED)
Ugh.

                    BERNARD
Are these from this year?

He holds BEACH PHOTOS of Brad and Dawn, who snatches them.

                     BRAD
Last year. We went to St. Barts.

                    BERNARD
How about this year?

                     BRAD
We didn't go on a trip this year.

                    BERNARD
How come?

                     BRAD
A lotta work. Too busy.

                    BERNARD
Too busy for a vacation?

(CONTINUED)

CONTINUED: (2)

                    DAWN (CRYING)
          Why are you involved with this? You
          don't believe in therapy.

                    BRAD
          I don't see this as therapy. I'm
          pro-active, these people are action-
          oriented. It's like the company
          retreat at Hiltonhead when we did
          the trust thing, the paragliding.
          Everything lined up nice. It seemed
          like they were helping Albert, they
          could help me, help the Open
          Spaces.

                    DAWN
          What are you talking about?

                    VIVIAN
          He did say in his application that
          he felt exhausted from having to
          charm everyone constantly, but he
          doesn't see an alternative,
          because --

She flips through the pages of a little note pad:

                    BERNARD (READS OVER VIVIAN'S SHOULDER)
          Quote, "You need to get people to
          like you to be successful and get
          things done in this world,"
          unquote.

                    DAWN (TRYING TO BE CHEERY)
          Duh. Brad likes to be charming, it
          comes naturally. Except in the
          morning when he's Mr. Grumpus.
          (giggles)

                    BRAD (CHUCKLING TO DETECTIVES)
          Hey, I only put those things in the
          garbage for you as a joke.

                    DAWN (LAUGHING/STILL CRYING)
          That's so funny, see? That's crazy.
          He's a prankster. That's Brad! He
          likes to make people laugh!
          Seriously, seriously, that's what
          you're picking up on.

                    VIVIAN
          Mmm. That's almost worse, isn't it?

(CONTINUED)

CONTINUED: (3)

> BERNARD (WRITING)
> Backdoor way to charm. Joking as
> disguised request for approval.
> Joke, love me, joke, love me.

> VIVIAN
> Ms. Campbell, how have you felt
> about being pretty?

> DAWN
> Oh, please, I was never the pretty
> girl. Yes, that's changed at
> Huckabees, but I still don't think
> of myself as being THAT pretty, I
> just hafta keep up with this
> gorgeous hottie.

She rubs Brads arms and shoulders.

> BERNARD
> How's the sex?

> VIVIAN
> Yeah, how's the sex?

> BRAD
> Come on, guys, that's
> private.

> DAWN
> That's gross.

> VIVIAN (LOOKING AT NOTES)
> Preliminary surveillance indicates
> it's been infrequent and short,
> eight to nine minutes typically.

> DAWN
> Surveillance! You've watched us?

> VIVIAN
> No, just listened.

> BRAD
> That is out of line. We have never
> had a problem in that department.

> VIVIAN
> Well, eight to nine minutes.

> DAWN
> It's quantity not quality.

> BRAD
> She means quality not quantity.

CONTINUED: (4)

                    DAWN (LAUGHING NERVOUSLY)
          I know, I was only joking.

                    BERNARD
          Were you?

                    BRAD
          We're not gonna discuss this now.

                    DAWN (LAUGHING NERVOUSLY)
          We're private about our seven
          minutes of heaven!

                    BRAD
          It's longer than that, Dawn.

                    DAWN (LAUGHING NERVOUSLY)
          Eight minutes of heaven! It's not
          quality, it's quantity!

                    BRAD
          Dawn.

Dawn continues to laugh manically.

                    BRAD (CONT'D)
          You oughta see her after a couple
          of margaritas.

                    DAWN (LAUGHING NERVOUSLY)
          Oh, my God, I'm crying. Honey!
          (whispering to Brad) Why did you
          write this poem and how come we
          can't discuss these things
          ourselves? Where is this
          relationship going?

                    BRAD
          What's so great about marriage and
          kids? Isn't there an overpopulation
          problem?

              VIVIAN   BERNARD
Whoa.   That came out of left field.

                    BRAD (CONT'D)
          Why is having kids the ultimate
          performance for successful people?

                                        (CONTINUED)

> DAWN
> It doesn't have to be a
> performance, I mean, we don't have
> to have kids, it could be just us,
> you know, jet skiing, whatever, we
> can think about kids or not --

> BRAD
> This isn't what I hired you for.

> DAWN
> What did you hire them for?

Dawn looks at Brad, who looks down at the floor.

> BRAD
> Well. I have a meeting to go to.

THEY ALL LOOK AT HIM, NOT BUDGING. DOORBELL RINGS. BRAD
EXITS.

> CUT TO:

BERNARD AND VIVIAN PEER THROUGH KITCHEN WINDOW AS BRAD GREETS
BUSINESSMEN OUTSIDE.

> CUT TO:

INT. KITCHEN - SAME DAY

> DAWN (NERVOUS) (O.S.)
> Would you like some tea?

> BERNARD (O.S.)
> With a little lemon.

> DAWN
> So, I've never really done anything
> like this before. Where would we
> start?

The only sound is Bernard's teaspoon stirring his tea as he
and Vivian stare intensely at Dawn, who looks vulnerable.

EXT. MEADOW - DAY

ALBERT AND TOMMY SIT AT AN OLD PICNIC TABLE; ALBERT SMASHES A
LARGE BALL INTO TOMMY'S FACE, CATERINE WATCHES FROM A
DISTANCE.

> TOMMY
> Now.

CONTINUED:

Albert SMASHES THE BALL INTO TOMMY'S FACE.

                    TOMMY (CONT'D)
          Now. (ball smashes into Tommy's
          face) Now. (again)

Tommy stares, trips out. Nods slowly.

                    ALBERT
          Did you get it?

                    TOMMY
          Yeah, that's it, I felt it. It's
          hard to describe.

                    CATERINE
          Very good. Your turn.

Albert looks a little scared as Tommy takes the ball.

                    ALBERT
          Now.

Tommy smashes him in the face, knocking him over.

                    ALBERT (CONT'D)
          Not so hard.

                    TOMMY
          Sorry.

                    ALBERT
          NOW (smashed), Now, (smashed) NOW.
          (again)

Tommy stops and watches as Albert trips on this, savoring it.

                    TOMMY
          Did you get it?

                    ALBERT
          Yeah, you stop thinking.

                    TOMMY
          YES! It's fantastic!

                    CATERINE (SMILES)
          Very, very good.

CONTINUED: (2)

                    ALBERT
          It's like I'm here, but almost not
          here, there's just ... I don't know
          what this is. Do it again.

Tommy hits him with the ball, induces another trance in
Albert.

                    ALBERT (CONT'D)
          It's like being a rock or a dish of
          mold. We're no different than
          whatever else is around, so we're
          free to just exist --

                    TOMMY (HAPPY)
          This is the answer! We should just
          be this all day every day.

                    ALBERT (HAPPY)
          Yeah, that's the answer.

                    CATHERINE (TAKING THE BIG BALL)
          Careful, my young students. You
          cannot stay in this state all day.

                    TOMMY
          Why not?

                    ALBERT
          Yeah, why not?

                    CATERINE
          It is inevitable that you are drawn
          back into human drama, desire,
          suffering, everything that exists
          in this imperfect world.

                    ALBERT
          Shit.

                    TOMMY
          So we get drawn back into drama and
          how important we think that is, we
          do crazy things, THEN, we have to
          go back to the ball thing and get
          the freedom of just being like a
          dish of mold --

                    CATERINE
          And then back to the drama, the
          suffering --

CONTINUED: (3)

> ALBERT
> Kind of a crappy deal.

> CATERINE (CHEERFUL)
> Exactement ca, an absurd theatrical
> we must play out, back and forth
> from pure being to human suffering.

> TOMMY
> But isn't the drama and suffering
> less if you do the ball thing every
> day?

> CATERINE
> Don't call it "ball thing" -- call
> it Pure Being.

> ALBERT
> Wouldn't the Pure Being ball thing
> make day-to-day suffering easier?

> TOMMY CORN
> Yeah.

> CATERINE (FRUSTRATED)
> No, it doesn't.

> TOMMY CORN
> You're wrong. We're gonna do this
> every day. We'll show you. It'll
> make it easier.

> CATERINE
> I'll prove it to you.

> TOMMY CORN
> How?

HER FOOT, UNDER THE PICNIC TABLE THEY SIT AT, GOES INTO
ALBERT'S CROTCH, SENSUOUSLY.

> CUT TO:

Albert's expression changes as her foot massages his balls.

> CATERINE
> Human drama is inevitable.
> Suffering cannot be diminished. You
> cannot escape, Tommy, you'll see.
> (MORE)

CONTINUED:

                    CATERINE (CONT'D)
          Existence is a cruel joke that
          entices in the form of exalted
          desire --

                    ALBERT
          Absurd theatre of desire -- aaghhh.
          (aroused)

                    TOMMY
          I know buddy, it hurts. It's
          painful.

Caterine stands up. Albert stands, follows her off-camera
right, leaving Tommy alone.

                    CATERINE
          Wait here.

                    TOMMY
          Where are you going?

                    CATERINE (WALKING AWAY)
          To meditate on desire and
          suffering.

                    TOMMY
          Can I come?

                    CATERINE
          No.

                    TOMMY CORN
          OK, I'll see you in a little bit?
          We'll do more pure being...?

Albert looks at Tommy as he walks backward, as if pulled
helplessly against his will.

                    ALBERT
          I hope so.

Tommy stares after them, eyebrows raised with worry, anger,
loneliness --

                    TOMMY CORN (MUTTERING TO HIMSELF)
          Fucking leave me.

                                        CUT TO:

EXT. HUTCHINSON MARSH - DAY

Albert and Caterine jog through the woods holding hands. HE
DROPS TO HIS KNEES, THEN HIS BELLY, CARESSING ROOTS AND
EARTH. SHE HOLDS HIS HAND. HE RUBS HER LEGS WITH LEAVES,
SHOVES HANDFULS UNDER HER DRESS.

She tilts her head back and chokes out sounds of pleasure.

                    CATERINE VAUBAN (EYES CLOSED)
          Aaahhhhgggg ca gaghhhhhkk aaagh.

He pulls her to the ground, where he rubs dirt and leaves on
her face, her breasts. They kiss, stare at each other.
Slowly, she dunks his face repeatedly in a mud puddle.

                    ALBERT (SLOWLY DUNKED IN PUDDLE)
          Augh... Augh... Augh.

He kisses her passionately, then pushes her face into the mud
puddle. She pulls up. They kiss passionately.

                                        CUT TO:

THEY FUCK ON A ROCK.

EXT. BRAD'S HOUSE - ANOTHER MORNING

Brad walks out of his kitchen door into the driveway and
tosses ROLLED-UP ARCHITECTURAL PLANS into his BMW SUV, he
turns to see DAWN WALK OUT. SHE HAS UGLIFIED HERSELF, NO MAKE
UP, BED-HEAD, SUPER BAGGY OVERALLS AND WORKBOOTS. Brad stares
at her, upset.

                    DAWN (EATING MINI OREOS)
          What?

                    BRAD (HOLDING ARCHITECTURAL PLANS)
          You can't keep going to work like
          that.

                    UGLIFIED DAWN
          This is me.

                    BRAD
          That is not you.

                    UGLIFIED DAWN
          Me and Daryl made some thirty-
          second spots Marty's gonna love.

INSERT: UGLIFIED DAWN COMMERCIAL

                                        (CONTINUED)

CONTINUED:

                                  BRAD
MARTY WILL HATE THEM, DAWN.

                           UGLIFIED DAWN
You can't deal with my infinite
nature, can you?

                                  BRAD
That is SO not true, wait, what
does that mean?

                     UGLIFIED DAWN (PATRONIZING)
We have talked about your intimacy
problem, what's the core of it?
Intimacy is a combo of infinites.

                                  BRAD
I'm definitely gonna have an
intimacy problem if you look like
this all the time.

                           UGLIFIED DAWN
It's only been a week.

                                  BRAD
One day is too much. People at the
office are freaking out.

                           UGLIFIED DAWN
You could get free, Brad, but you
think you have to be Superman in
control and that means YOU are the
source, instead of PART of the
infinite, that makes it too hard
for us.

                                  BRAD
STOP TALKING TO ME LIKE THAT.

                           UGLIFIED DAWN
You hired the detectives.

                                  BRAD
You don't have to listen to every
word they say.

                           UGLIFIED DAWN
How am I supposed to know which
parts to listen to?

                              BRAD (MAD)
BECAUSE I'M TELLING YOU.

CONTINUED: (2)

                    UGLIFIED DAWN
          It's confusing.

Brad gets into his BMW SUV, disgusted. DAWN PUTS ON AN AMISH-
STYLE BONNET.

                    BRAD (IN HIS CAR)
          Take that off.

                    UGLIFIED DAWN
          Can I have my car keys, please?

                    BRAD
          NO. Stay home till you dress
          normal. Don't come to the office.

Brad drives off, leaving Dawn standing there.

INT. HUCKABEES STUDIO - DAY

Dawn walks onto the COLORFUL COMMERCIAL SET holding her
script wearing her baggy grey overalls, work boots, no make-
up, an Amish bonnet. HEATHER, a pretty younger blond in a
sexy outfit, is there. She sits on set holding her script,
ready to tape, when DARYL, the engineer, comes into the
control room. THEY SPEAK THROUGH INTERCOMS.

                    UGLIFIED DAWN (WARM)
          Hey, Daryl, how are ya?

                    DARYL
          Great, honey. Let's make a
          commercial.

                    DARYL (CONT'D)
          This is Heather, Dawn.

                    UGLIFIED DAWN (WARM)
          Hi, Heather. Welcome to our family.

                    HEATHER (GIGGLING)
          It's so weird to meet my voice. I
          love your work by the way.

                    UGLIFIED DAWN (CONFUSED)
          Thanks. This script only has my
          lines, and I don't see another
          character here, so...

                    HEATHER (LAUGHING NERVOUSLY)
          She's the voice, I'm the face.

                                        (CONTINUED)

CONTINUED:

                         DARYL (CHUCKLES)
        More than a face, sweetheart.

                    HEATHER (WIGGLES HER HIPS)
        All this and brains, too.

DAWN LOOKS POWDERED.

INT. HUCKABEES CONFERENCE ROOM - DAY

Brad and the TWO EXECUTIVES review a seating plan for the
OPEN SPACES BENEFIT.

                  DEXICORP EXECUTIVE (TEXAS TWANG)
        When Garth headlined our Dallas
        benefit, we seated the $10,000 VIP
        donors in front, and right behind
        was a --

Dawn runs up to the conference room in her bonnet and
overalls and bangs on the glass asking where Marty is. Brad
and the executives look concerned.

INT. HUCKABEES OPEN OFFICE FLOOR - CONTINUOUS

Dawn storms through as Huckabees PEOPLE work and bustle
about. A LARGE TV plays a tape loop of Heather lip-synching
to Dawn's voice.

                  HEATHER WITH DAWN'S VOICE (VIDEO LOOP)
        ...Welcome to the Huckabees Open
        Spaces Gala Event. Huckabees
        pledges to help save our
        environment. One world. One Store.
        Huckabees, the Everything Store...
        Welcome to the Huckabees Open...

Dawn passes by the TV and walks up to Marty.

                  UGLIFIED DAWN
        Why don't you like my spots?

                  MARTY
        Honey, this look is hurting you and
        it's hurting Huckabees.

                  UGLIFIED DAWN
        This is myself.

                  MARTY
        Then you won't speak at the benefit
        as yourself. That is not Huckabees.

CONTINUED:

> UGLIFIED DAWN
> I am Huckabees.

> MARTY
> Not in that bonnet.

> UGLIFIED DAWN
> It's in my eyes, Marty. It's like
> that story of the cave.

> MARTY
> What in God's name is happening to
> you? We pulled you out of a mall,
> made you a national icon, you've
> been given so much by Huckabees.

> UGLIFIED DAWN (PISSED)
> FUCKabees.

She storms out. Brad comes in, flustered.

> MARTY
> Bradley, there are board members
> here and it's not gonna look too
> good for our new corporate guy.

> BRAD
> I got corporate?

> MARTY
> Yes, you got corporate. Now go and
> get corporate and contain her.

INT. HALLWAY - CONTINUOUS

Brad bursts into the hall and Dawn is nowhere to be seen. He
opens doors to empty offices on the hall, till he finds Dawn
lying down on a desk with an eye mask covering her eyes.

INT. EMPTY OFFICE - CONTINUOUS

> BRAD (AGITATED)
> What are you doing? What are you
> doing to us?

> UGLIFIED DAWN
> I'm in my tree, I'm talking to the
> Dixie Chicks and they're making me
> feel better.

(CONTINUED)

CONTINUED:

                    BRAD
        Well, I think the Dixie Chicks
        would like you to know that I just
        got promoted.

                    UGLIFIED DAWN
        What?

                    BRAD
        VP for Public Affairs. I got
        corporate, Dawn. I'm sorry you had
        to go through all this. It's for
        the greater good. I went to the
        detectives to shake Albert out of
        the Coalition, I admit that.

                    UGLIFIED DAWN
        This doesn't make sense.

                    BRAD
        Sweetheart, you're mixing yourself
        up. Listen, you're mixing it all
        up.

                    UGLIFIED DAWN   (CONFUSED)
        Wait a second, do you even care
        about the marsh and the woods?

                    BRAD
        Yes, I care about the marsh and the
        woods. Albert was never gonna save
        the marsh his way, you don't go
        through the back door, with a poem
        and a bonnet like that, you go
        through the front door with a tie
        and you OWN the marsh and the
        woods. That's how you're gonna
        save them. Let's celebrate.
        You want some new clothes? I'll
        get you whatever you want. What do
        you need?

                    UGLIFIED DAWN   (SMILES)
        I don't know.

                    BRAD
        Pedicure?

                    UGLIFIED DAWN
        But do I have to be pretty all the
        time?

                                        (CONTINUED)

CONTINUED: (2)

                         BRAD
          Well, you have a choice.

                    UGLIFIED DAWN
          But no, it's not a choice. I do
          have to be pretty.

                         BRAD
          Well, I'm pretty sure the Dixie
          Chicks would want you to spread
          your love here where you can, at
          Huckabees.

                    UGLIFIED DAWN
          Right, that's good. You know
          what....you got Albert fired.

                         BRAD
          Stay positive. Bermuda, jet skis,
          piña coladas, all right? When you
          leave the office, will you leave
          through the back door 'cause you
          don't look so good today.

                         DAWN
          OK.

Dawn looks powdered and Brad leans over to kiss her.

                                        CUT TO:

EXT. BURNING HOUSE - DAY

TOMMY DISINTERESTEDLY PUTTING OUT THE FIRE. DRIFTS OFF THE
HOUSE WITH THE HOSE. OTHER FIREMEN COME AT HIM AND HE SPRAYS
THEM.

                                        CUT TO:

TOMMY SITS ALONE ON THE ROCK IN HIS FUNERAL UNIFORM, LONELY.
HE SMACKS HIMSELF IN THE FACE WITH THE ZEN BALL, THEN KICKS
IT AWAY, DEJECTED.

INT. CATERINE'S HOTEL ROOM - DAY

ALBERT LYING ON THE BED WITH HIS EYES CLOSED.

INT. ALBERT'S MIND

Caterine sitting in the tree with a forest in the background.

                                        (CONTINUED)

CONTINUED:

                     CATERINE VAUBAN (FRENCH/ENGLISH)
         The woods are hopeless, don't waste
         your time, they will be destroyed.
         So will the marsh. It is a losing
         game mankind has played for more
         than a century. Sadness is what you
         are, do not deny it. The universe
         is a lonely place, a painful place.
         This is what we can share, between
         us, period.

BRAD AND DAWN APPEAR RIDING A JET SKI. Albert HACKS AT IT. A
BUCKETFUL OF WATER FROM NOWHERE SPLASHES IN ALBERT'S FACE.

INT. CATERINE'S RAMADA INN ROOM - CONTINUOUS

Caterine, wet from the shower with a towel around her, stands
with AN EMPTY GLASS OF WATER SHE HAS JUST THROWN IN ALBERT'S
FACE AS HE LIES ON THE BED.

                     CATERINE VAUBAN
         What are you doing?

He looks at her guiltily, wipes his face.

                     CATERINE VAUBAN (CONT'D)
         You told me you were done with this
         stupid practice.

                     ALBERT
         Why can't I do it?

                     CATERINE VAUBAN
         Because it is a fantasy. Do you
         want to live a fake life?

                     ALBERT
         I can mix some of your thing with
         theirs.

                     CATERINE VAUBAN
         NO, YOU CAN'T.

                     ALBERT
         Why not?

                     CATERINE VAUBAN
      BECAUSE THEY ARE COMPLETELY
      DIFFERENT, AND THEIRS IS A LIE. FOR
      THE LAST TIME, FORGET THE TREE
      FANTASY.
         (MORE)

CONTINUED:

                    CATERINE VAUBAN (CONT'D)
              AND AS FOR BRAD, YOU MUST DO TO HIM
              WHAT HE DID TO YOU FOR REAL AND --

KNOCK AT THE DOOR. TOMMY ENTERS, LOOKING WOUNDED.

                    TOMMY CORN
          You ditched me. First my family
          and now you guys. She's my
          teacher, too, Albert.

                    ALBERT
          She's still your teacher, too,
          Tommy.

                    TOMMY CORN
          No, it's all different now. I
          thought we were a Platonic trio. No
          sick sex dance. You said that was
          bullshit.

                    CATERINE VAUBAN (PUTTING ON LOTION)
          Learn from this, Tommy. Painful
          truth. I warned you. Human drama.

                    TOMMY CORN
          Is that why you're doing this? To
          teach me?

                    ALBERT
          Yeah, is that why you're doing
          this? To teach him?

                    CATERINE VAUBAN
          There are unique moments when two
          people share the deep sorrow of
          existence.

                    ALBERT
          All right, that's what I wanted to
          hear.

He drapes himself across her back as she sits.

                    TOMMY CORN
          How can you believe that bullshit,
          Albert?

                    ALBERT
          Tommy, I'm sorry this just
          happened. You can still be my
          Other, I think, right?

                                            (CONTINUED)

CONTINUED: (2)

                    TOMMY CORN
          Shut up, Albert. I brought you
          here. I wanted you to share *la
          force* with you and you ruined it.
          You fell in love.

                    CATERINE VAUBAN
          Do not defile it with cliche. It is
          unnameable.

                    TOMMY CORN
          I reject "unnameable." It leaves me
          out.

He PUNCHES OVER A LAMP and leaves.

INT. BRAD'S OFFICE - DAY

Brad grins smugly as he sits opposite Bernard, who faces the
desk, while Vivian sits on the window sill.

          BERNARD   BRAD (SIMULTANEOUSLY MIMICS)
Let's start with the method --   Let's start with the method --

          BERNARD   BRAD (SIMULTANEOUSLY MIMICS)
We'd like to discuss --   We'd like to discuss --

          BERNARD   BRAD (SIMULTANEOUSLY MIMICS)
What are you doing?   What are you doing?

Bernard and Vivian look at him mildly irritated.

                    BRAD (CHUCKLING)
          I'm joking around, guys. But
          seriously, I want to quit this
          process with you. Nothing personal,
          I'm just over it.

They look at him. He continues to smile warmly.

                    BERNARD
          You can't quit until the case is
          closed.

                    BRAD
          I can fire you.

                    BERNARD AND VIVIAN
          No, you can't.

Bernard produces the telephone book-thick contract and plops
it on the desk, putting on his reading glasses.

                                              (CONTINUED)

CONTINUED:

                    BERNARD (READS)
          Paragraph 201: "Neither client nor
          detective may terminate case prior
          to resolution as defined by
          paragraph 314, subclause D," which
          states --

                    BRAD
          I'll just go to a lawyer or maybe
          even the FBI, how about that?

                    VIVIAN
          Go ahead.

                    BRAD
          I'll do it, I'm not kidding.

                    VIVIAN
          This is how it works, Brad --

She crosses the room confidently.

                    VIVIAN (CONT'D)
          You go to the police, you tell them
          you went to the existential
          detectives. They ask why, you say
          for some personal problems, or
          because you wanted to work the
          politics at your corporation by
          rattling Albert Markovksi --

                    BRAD
          I never told you that --

                    BERNARD
          Give us a little credit.

                    VIVIAN
          So the police talk to Huckabees.
          The board hears rising star Brad
          Stand has weird existential issues,
          or fakes them --

                    BERNARD
          Which is odd.

                    VIVIAN
          And your girlfriend, the Voice of
          Huckabees, has been dressing like
          an Amish bag lady --

CONTINUED: (2)

                    BRAD
          OK, I get it.

                    BERNARD
          Suddenly your star isn't rising so
          much anymore. It's sinking.

                    BRAD
          I said OK, Bernie, relax.

                    VIVIAN
          Passive aggressive.

                    BRAD
          Shut up.

                    BERNARD
          Aggressive.

                    VIVIAN
          Does Dawn want to quit?

                    BRAD
          Dawn's into this crap for real,
          it's the stupidest thing I've seen
          in my life.

                    BERNARD
          Shall we get back to your case?

                    BRAD
          What choice do I have?

                    BERNARD
          Our staff did a little field work
          in Cleveland.

                    BRAD
          You saw my family --

                    BERNARD
          Yeah.

He has a FAMILY PHOTO of BRAD'S PERFECT-LOOKING PARENTS.

                    VIVIAN
          Mommy and Daddy look awesome, but
          this guy...

Points to BRAD'S FAT BROTHER, STEVE.

                                        (CONTINUED)

CONTINUED: (3)

> BERNARD (A "YOU LOSE" HONK)
> Bwa bwaa. He doesn't look so good.

BRAD SEEMS TO START CRYING. THE DETECTIVES WATCH, THEN BRAD
LAUGHS MOCKINGLY.

> BRAD (PUSHING HIS BROTHER'S PHOTO)
> You gotta be kidding me, he weighs
> 250 and talks about geckos all the
> time, do you get off on that?

> VIVIAN
> I thought he was a sweet, sensitive
> young man.

> BRAD
> You talked to my brother?

> BERNARD
> On the phone, yes.

> BRAD
> If he's so sensitive, why doesn't
> he lose about 70 pounds and stop
> talking about geckos? Maybe he'll
> make some friends.

> VIVIAN (REFERS TO NOTES)
> Your brother feels like you're
> ashamed of him.

> BRAD
> He's a sad guy, what can I do?

> BERNARD
> Are you sympathetic to him?

> BRAD
> Are you kidding? I gave him a car.
> I'm a great older brother.

> VIVIAN
> He wishes you'd listen to him more.

> BRAD
> About what? Geckos? Maybe he should
> listen to me more.

> VIVIAN (REFERS TO NOTES)
> You like to tell several stories
> over and over again.

                                      BRAD
That's not true. I'm not boring.

                                 BERNARD
Like the mayonnaise story.

Vivian HITS A BUTTON ON A TAPE PLAYER, A TAPE PLAYS.
VIVIAN'S VOICE ON THE TAPE ANNOUNCES DATE AND PLACE.

                            TAPE OF BRAD
May 18th, Sales Meeting. "Shania's
there, promoting her apparel,
right? It's four o'clock and she's
starving. She hates mayonnaise,
allergic to it, so I order a ton of
tuna-fish sandwiches. "Back then
that's all she's eating, tuna fish,
NO MAYO, Darlene --"

Brad can't help laughing now as he hears his own story.

                       TAPE OF BRAD (CONT'D)
June 5th, driving range. "No joke.
We gave her chicken salad once, she
threw up in the back of a limo --"

Laughter on the tape.

                       TAPE OF BRAD (CONT'D)
June 30th, the lake. "Shania's
there, promoting her apparel,
right? And she's starving --"

LAUGHTER on the tape. Tape continues in this vein. Brad sits
with his arms folded on his chest, pissed. Story ends. Tape
stops and rewinds. Pause.

                            VIVIAN
Why do you think you tell the mayo
story so much?

                               BRAD
I don't know. Why?

                             BERNARD
It's propaganda.

                               BRAD
For mayonnaise?

CONTINUED: (5)

>   BERNARD
> For you.

>   VIVIAN
> Specifically, that you are
> impressive for being close to
> Shania, yet strong enough to pull
> something on her.

>   BERNARD
> You're a "funny guy, a good guy."

>   VIVIAN
> And you keep everyone laughing so
> you won't "be depressed."

>   BRAD (REVEALING)
> What's so great about depression?

>   BERNARD
> Nothing, unless it holds the key to
> something you compulsively avoid so
> it will never be examined or felt,
> hence your behavior becomes
> repetitive, like the story.

>   VIVIAN
> Like the story.

>   BERNARD
> Like the story.

>   VIVIAN
> Like the story.

>   BERNARD
> Like the story.

>   BRAD
> Shut up.

They look at him.

>   VIVIAN
> Are you really being yourself? What
> would happen if you didn't tell the
> stories?

>   BRAD   BERNARD & VIVIAN (MIMICS)
> How am I not myself?   How am I not myself?

CONTINUED: (6)

Brad stares at the detectives silently. Bobby opens the door; Brad leaves. The detectives watch him go impassively.

INT. OUTSIDE EXECUTIVE MEN'S ROOM - DAY

Brad walks down the hall with a loop of Bernard playing in his head. SEVERAL SECRETARIES pass him, each glancing longingly.

LOOP IN BRAD'S HEAD: "How am I not myself? How am I not myself?..."

INT. HUCKABEES CORPORATE CENTER - EXECUTIVE MEN'S ROOM - DAY

Brad walks into the bathroom. He chews his lips in anxiety, looks at himself in the mirror, washes his face.

>   BRAD
>   BAAAAHHH. Grrahhh.

But he looks vulnerable again, deep pain in his eyes. The door opens, Brad HIDES IN A STALL. Marty walks in, whistling.

>   MARTY
>   How do you like the corporate men's
>   room, Bradley?

>   BRAD (O.S.)
>   Friggin' awesome, Marty.

>   MARTY
>   You wanna hear something funny?
>   The Dundalee cups are blowing out
>   of the sunbelt franchises. How's
>   that for super weird? That's a
>   good thing to bring to the table,
>   right? You are just what the
>   doctor ordered my friend. Right?

>   BRAD (O.S.)
>   Right on.

>   MARTY
>   Well, let's go, dude. I'm going to
>   introduce you to the board of
>   directors, my friend.

>   CUT TO:

INT. HUCKABEES CORPORATE CONFERENCE ROOM - DAY

Brad sits at a table with 12 OLDER, ELITE CORPORATE
EXECUTIVES, plus the two bald Dexicorp executives.

                    CORPORATE GUY 1
          Legal says it's a problem.

                    CORPORATE GUY 2
          I disagree. We give 'em the Salmon
          Stripper, say it's a Bass Basher,
          they can't read English anyway.

                    CORPORATE GUY 1
          How about the Tuna Tornado?

                    CORPORATE GUY 2
          There you go. Legal can cover that.

                    CORPORATE GUY 3
          Hey, I saw Shania in our studio
          getting ready for tonight.

                    CORPORATE GUY 2
          That benefit is sweet. I already
          saw an article that makes us sound
          like save the baby seals and the
          flowers and shit.

                    CORPORATE GUY 1
          You actually gonna save this marsh?

                    DEXICORP EXECUTIVE
          We worked it out.

                    BRAD
          I'll make the announcement tonight
          at the benefit.

                    MARTY (CHUCKLING)
          Brad's got a fantastic Shania story
          about tuna fish.

All eyes turn to Brad.

                    BRAD
          I don't want to tell that story.

                    MARTY
          What?

CONTINUED:

                    BRAD
I don't wanna tell that story,
Marty.

                    MARTY
Come on. You and Shania are
downtown in the loop, you're
opening a store and all of a sudden
she gets?...

Marty looks at Brad as Brad just sits rocking back and forth
hugging himself.

                MARTY (CONT'D)
She gets?

                    BRAD
Hungry.

                    MARTY
Really hungry, right. And so, you
order?...

                BRAD (STRUGGLING)
Tuna sandwiches.

                    MARTY
Tuna fish. But you realize that
she's allergic to --

Brad STOPS, squeezes his lips shut.

                BRAD (STRUGGLING)
Ahh, no, Marty --

                    MARTY
Come on, she's allergic to what?

Brad hugs his arms, rocks in his chair and spits up in his
hand.

                MARTY (CONT'D)
Why don't you and me go outside and
have a talk, OK?

                BRAD (GETTING UP)
I'll be back in five minutes.

                    MARTY
Sure we do, come on.

CONTINUED: (2)

              CORPORATE GUY 1
       Is this guy gonna put a bonnet on?

              CORPORATE GUY 2
       What the fuck was that?

CUT TO: ALBERT EYES CLOSED LEANING AGAINST WALL

FLASHBACK: Brad tossing Albert a Huckabees button and Albert
shaking hands with Brad.

ALBERT SCREAMS IN FRUSTRATION ON THE ROCK.

              ALBERT
       I hate the day I ever met that
       phoney, seducing bastard! I hate
       that I sold myself out to him!

He grabs a big lighter and a magazine with an ad for jet skis
on the back, plus a Huckabees publicity photo of Brad at a
ribbon cutting -- and he torches them.

              CATERINE (O.S.)
       BURN THE FAKERY OF YOURSELF! FREE
       YOURSELF FOR REAL.

              ALBERT
       Yeah, we're gonna burn him where it
       hurts, like you said.

              CATERINE
       Superb. Sublime! FOR REAL.

INT. FIREHOUSE - DAY

Tommy sits unshaven alone on a couch in the dark watching
monster trucks. THE ALARM SOUNDS. Tommy gets on his bike to
ride.

              FIREMAN 2
       You're gonna ride on the truck like
       everyone else.

              TOMMY CORN
       Get on the bike.

              FIREMAN 2
       Truck.

              TOMMY CORN
       Bike.

EXT. SUBURBAN STREET - DAY

Tommy rides his bike fast. Turns a corner. Rides more.

EXT. BRAD'S SUBURBAN HOUSE - DAY

Tommy turns into the driveway. The house is smoking slightly.
A couple of neighbors stand near the yard, watching. Tommy
waits in the driveway, looks at his watch, parks his bike.

EXT. ROUTE 4 - CONTINUOUS

THE FIRETRUCK IS STUCK IN A MASSIVE TRAFFIC JAM, HONKING. Ten
cars away, BRAD'S SUV is stuck in traffic.

EXT. BRAD'S HOUSE - DAY

TOMMY walks INTO THE HOUSE.

INT. BRAD'S HOUSE - DAY

Tommy wanders through the slightly smoky rooms. He gets to
UGLIFIED DAWN, WHO IS UNCONSCIOUS ON THE FLOOR. HE SHAKES
HER. THEY STARE AT EACH OTHER AS SURPRISE TURNS INTO
UNDERSTANDING. SHE KISSES TOMMY PASSIONATELY. They continue
kissing until they pass out.

                                        CUT TO:

EXT. BRAD'S SUBURBAN HOUSE

The firemen carry Tommy and Dawn to an ambulance.

EXT. BRAD'S HOUSE, HIDDEN IN THE BUSHES

Caterine and Albert lie on their backs in some bushes, a
GASOLINE CAN NEAR THEM.

                    CATERINE VAUBAN (LYING ON HER BACK)
               Creation destruction creation
               destruction creation destruction
               creation destruction creation --

Albert peers through bushes and sees Brad getting out of his
BMW SUV, frazzled and upset. THE DETECTIVES' CITROEN PULLS UP
BEHIND BRAD'S BMW.

FROM ALBERT'S POV: Brad sees one remaining firetruck as he
walks across his now torn-up lawn to the CHARRED REMAINS OF
HIS TWO JET SKIS. He falls to his knees, CRYING.

                                              (CONTINUED)

CONTINUED:

> BRAD (KNEELING, CRYING)
> Why? I'm lost in the wilderness.
> I'm lost.

He slowly claws at the lawn in agony. Vivian and Bernard
stand watching him cry.

> VIVIAN
> We can help you, Brad.

He looks up, imploring, tearful, vulnerable, a lost child.

> BRAD (LOOKS UP, TEARFUL)
> My life...I'm lost...I'll go with
> you (clutches at dirt and grass)...

> VIVIAN
> We can help you, Brad.

> BRAD
> I...need to go to the
> benefit...don't tell anybody...

Bernard and Vivian nod sympathetically.

> BRAD (CRYING, LOST) (CONT'D)
> OK...OK...Don't tell anybody I
> cried and, I don't care, tell
> everybody, no, please don't tell
> anybody, let me just be with you.
> No, that looks bad. Who cares? I'll
> go with you --

CATERINE STANDS IN THE BUSHES AND TAKES BRAD'S POLAROID.

> BRAD (CONT'D)
> NOBODY SEES THAT PICTURE! NOBODY
> SEES THAT! (addressing Vivian and
> Bernard) WHY DID YOU DO THAT?

> BERNARD
> We didn't do this, we would never
> do something like this.

> VIVIAN
> Never. Maybe sometimes, but we
> didn't do this.

CATERINE DROPS THE POLAROID ONTO ALBERT'S CHEST AS HE LIES
HIDDEN IN BUSHES AT HER FEET. HE HOLDS IT AND STARES AT IT.

                    BERNARD
        This isn't our thing --

                    VIVIAN
        That is her thing.

As Brad continues to cry off-screen, little cubes descend
from Albert's face onto the Polaroid to form a mosaic of
Albert's crying face on Brad's body. Camera zooms in on
picture as we dissolve to Albert's vision of him holding
hands with Brad, spinning. Dissolve back to Albert holding
picture -- a changed man.

                                        CUT TO:

                    BRAD
        All right, I'm gonna go to the
        benefit. Screw all you bastards!

                    BERNARD
        Brad, we didn't do this --

                    VIVIAN
        She did it, Brad!

                    CATERINE
        Yes I did!

Brad drives off in his SUV.

ALBERT STANDS AND ADDRESSES THE DETECTIVES AND CATERINE --

                    ALBERT
        That fire was a bitch-ass thing to
        do.

                    CATERINE
        No, it liberated you from Brad.

                    ALBERT (STILL A BIT BLISSED)
        Or did it bond me to Brad in the
        insanity of pain till I saw that
        I'm Brad and he's me?

                    VIVIAN
        Yes.

                    CATERINE
        No.

CONTINUED:

           ALBERT (TO CATERINE AND DETECTIVES)
You guys work together, don't you?

           VIVIAN
NO, we don't work together at all.

           ALBERT
Come on, it's a secret deal where
she picks us up where you leave
off, right? Then we come back to
you.

           BERNARD
Believe me, there's no secret deal.

           ALBERT
There should be, 'cause that's how
it works. You're too dark and
you're not dark enough.

They look flummoxed.

           ALBERT (CONT'D)
You three were close, maybe too
close? It went sour, and propelled
you into one extreme, and you into
the other: voila, two overlapping
fractured philosophies were born of
that pain.

He leaves.

           CATERINE
Albert.

           VIVIAN
Wait a second --

           BERNARD
What happened to him?

           CATERINE
I don't know.

EXT. ROUTE 4

Brad's car is stuck in a traffic jam. He gets out and starts
jogging along Route 4, past the traffic jam.

EXT. OMNI EXECUTIVE SUITES HOTEL - DAY

Albert pulls up on his bike, gives it to the valet as Brad
jogs up and heads inside, not seeing Albert, who turns to see
Brad going into the lobby and follows at a distance.

INT. OMNI EXECUTIVE SUITES HOTEL - CONTINUOUS

Brad walks into the lobby with Albert trailing behind him.
We watch Brad walk into an elevator with the doors closing on
him.

                              CUT TO:

ELEVATOR DOORS OPENING WITH ALBERT INSIDE.

INT. OUTSIDE THE 10TH-FLOOR BALLROOM

ALBERT GETS OFF THE ELEVATOR: band is heard from the nearby
ballroom. Albert walks past A GIANT TV SCREEN playing a tape
loop of HEATHER DANCING AND LIP-SYNCHING TO DAWN'S VOICE:

                    HEATHER WITH DAWN'S VOICE (VIDEO LOOP)
          ...Welcome to the Huckabees Open
          Spaces Gala Event. Huckabees
          pledges to help save our
          environment. One world. One Store.
          Huckabees, the Everything Store...
          Welcome to the Huckabees Open...

Albert sees Brad by the entrance of the ballroom. He quickly
hides behind a ficus and spies Brad as he stands at a WELCOME
TABLE manned by DARLENE, wearing a corsage, as she pleads to
Davy and a SECURITY GUARD to LET BRAD IN.

                    DARLENE (CRYING TO SECURITY GUARD)
          It's not right. Bradley is the
          reason this event even EXISTS.

                    DAVY
          Mr. Stand is on paid leave. He's
          not on the list.

                    DARLENE
          Why are you calling him Mr. Stand?
          This is Brad, people.

                    BRAD
          I just want to talk to Shania,
          guys. Come on. You gotta let me in.

                                          (CONTINUED)

CONTINUED:

                    DAVY
          SSSSSHHHH.

DAVY CLOSES THE DOORS TO THE BENEFIT FROM INSIDE. IT IS
SUDDENLY REALLY QUIET WITH THE DOORS CLOSED.

                    BRAD
          Go on in, Darlene.

                    DARLENE
          NO. Not without you.

                    BRAD (FRUSTRATED, PISSED)
          Go on, sweetheart I'll be OK.

Darlene looks sadly at Brad as she leaves him behind. DISTANT
MUFFLED APPLAUSE FROM INSIDE IS ALL THAT'S HEARD.

ALBERT watches Brad from behind the nearby ficus tree. SHANIA
TWAIN, in a cowboy hat, rushes by; Brad runs after her, grabs
her shoulder.

                    BRAD (CONT'D)
          SHANIA!

WHEN THE WOMAN TURNS AROUND, IT IS HEATHER, THE LIP-SYNCHER,
WHO LOOKS AT BRAD BLANKLY, TILL Mr. Nimieri and the Hooten
boy RUN UP TO HER WITH A COUPLE OF AUTOGRAPH HOUNDS. Heather
signs DAWN'S GLOSSY FOR Mr. Nimieri AND THE OTHERS.

                    MR. NIMIERI (EXCITED)
          FANTASTIC.

                    HEATHER
          These are still the old pictures.

                    AUTOGRAPH HOUND
          That's a rarity for sure.

ALBERT stares at Mr. Nimieri, yet again. Brad looks
crestfallen as he holds one of the glossies and stares at it.
Mr. Nimieri takes it from his hand. Brad looks from the
GLOSSY OF DAWN TO THE REAL DAWN, STANDING THERE HOLDING HANDS
WITH TOMMY, wearing her bonnet.

                    BRAD
          What is this, Dawn?

                    UGLIFIED DAWN
          Do you love me?

                                        (CONTINUED)

                        BRAD
          I think so.

                        UGLIFIED DAWN
          With the bonnet?

                        BRAD (STRUGGLING)
          Aahhhhh --

                        UGLIFIED DAWN (CRYING)
          It's over, Brad. I had a fire and
          almost died and when he came he
          almost died because he cares about
          the same things and that shows
          there's no nothing? Even when you
          die? And he likes my bonnet.

                        SECURITY GUARD
          We got a VIP function here and I
          need you all to leave the premises.
          (HE TURNS AROUND ADDRESSING ALBERT)
          The gentleman behind the bush, you
          have to leave also.

Albert steps out from behind the bushes. Brad walks to the
elevators with Tommy and Dawn and pushes the button. Albert
joins them. Awkward silence till the elevator arrives. Albert
and Brad get in, Tommy and Dawn do not.

INT. ELEVATOR - CONTINUOUS

TWO WOMEN CELLISTS IN GOWNS RIDE DOWN WITH BRAD AND ALBERT.

                        BRAD
          Did they let you into the benefit?

                        ALBERT
          I didn't even try.

They ride in silence.

                        ALBERT (CONT'D)
          I've thought of chopping your head
          off with a machete many times.

                        BRAD
          I've thought about hacking you up
          with an axe or smashing your face
          in with a baseball bat.

The elevator stops, CELLISTS HURRY OFF, DROPPING A CELLO. A
COUPLE IN A GOWN AND TUX stand outside the open doors.

                                              (CONTINUED)

CONTINUED:

                    GUY IN TUX
Are you going up?

                    ALBERT
We're going down.

                    GUY IN TUX
I think you're going up.

                BRAD (HOLDING THE DOORS)
Right you are, Sir, come on in --

He gallantly holds the doors for the COUPLE, lets the doors
close, BUT SOMEONE JAMS AN ARM THROUGH AND THE DOORS OPEN:
MARY JANE, ANGELA, HARRISON STAND THERE.

                  BRAD (CONT'D)
Jump on in, Mary Jane --

SHE SLAPS HIM HARD ACROSS THE FACE.

                  ANGELA FRANCO
BRADLEY, HOW COULD YOU DO SUCH A
THING!

                    BRAD
Wait a second, it's a win for us.

                MARY JANE HUTCHINSON
A DEXICORP MALL IN GRANDFATHER'S
WOODS IS HARDLY A WIN. THEY'RE
ALREADY SURVEYING FOR CONSTRUCTION.

                    BRAD
But I saved the marsh.

                  HARRISON
By giving them the woods!

THE ELEVATOR ALARM SOUNDS AS BRAD HOLDS THE DOOR OPEN.

                    GUY IN TUX
ARE WE GOING UP OR WHAT?

                  ANGELA FRANCO
YOU MADE HUCKABEES LOOK GOOD,
THAT'S ALL YOU DID.

                HARRISON (TO ALBERT)
HOW CAN YOU BE SO CALM? DID YOU
HEAR WHAT BRAD DID?

(CONTINUED)

CONTINUED: (2)

                    ALBERT
          Don't worry, I'm dealing with it.

Albert remains mysteriously calm. The alarm keeps ringing.

                    BRAD
          SIT DOWN WITH ME AND SHANIA AND
          YOU'LL SEE THIS IS A WIN FOR US --

                    ANGELA FRANCO
          SHANIA DOESN'T GIVE A SHIT!

                    BRAD
          Shania cares.

                    GUY IN TUX
          LET'S GO!

Brad lets the doors close on Angela. Alarm off. Elevator up.

                    ALBERT
          You sold out the woods, huh?

                    BRAD
          The mall's going to be very eco-
          friendly, we saved almost half the
          trees. YES, I sold out the woods. I
          DON'T KNOW. I thought it was good,
          we saved half of it.

Pause.

                    ALBERT
          I torched your jet skis.

                    BRAD
          My house?

                    ALBERT
          Your jet skis. It spread to the
          house, sorry.

The Tux Guy and Gown Woman look freaked out. ELEVATOR STOPS,
the couple gets off. TWO LADIES IN GOWNS get on.

                    LADY IN GOWN
          Going down?

Albert and Brad nod. Elevator DOWN. PAUSE. ALBERT PULLS OUT
THE POLAROID OF SAD BRAD.

(CONTINUED)

CONTINUED: (3)

> ALBERT
> Who is that, you or me?

> BRAD
> Give me that.

Albert holds it away, Brad starts angrily slamming Albert
repeatedly into the gown ladies. Albert and Brad fall to the
floor. Brad smushes Albert's face with his open hand.
Albert does the same to Brad.

> ALBERT
> You're only smushing yourself,
> Brad.

Brad starts shaking Albert in frustration. Elevator keeps
going down, then STOPS, doors open. SHANIA TWAIN STANDS
THERE.

> BRAD AND ALBERT (IN UNISON)
> Shania.

> SHANIA (PISSED, HITTING BRAD)
> Brad, do you realize when they
> destroy the woods, the average
> temperature of the marsh will rise
> five degrees and the entire food
> chain will be degraded, starting
> with the frogs? And I'm a
> vegetarian, I eat tofu tuna.

> BRAD
> With mayo, and you liked it.

Doors close on Shania, guys sit down. Elevator continues
down. Gown Ladies stare at Brad.

> BRAD (CONT'D)
> She knew my name.

> ALBERT
> SO WHAT if she knew your name?

> BRAD
> I was joking, man, come on.

Albert looks at him.

> BRAD (CONT'D)
> Yeah, OK, I'm caught up in that
> shit.

CONTINUED: (4)

                    ALBERT
          So am I, that's how I bought into
          you.

ELEVATOR OPENS:

                    ANGELA FRANCO (QUIETLY)
          I owe you an apology, Albert, we
          should've stayed with you.

                    ALBERT
          Thanks, Angela. I'll see you at
          Tuesday's meeting. We're gonna stop
          the bulldozers.

ELEVATOR DOORS CLOSE ON ANGELA ET. AL.

                    BRAD
          I don't have a job. I don't even
          know who I am.

                    ALBERT
          That's exactly how I felt. Try this
          lady.

HE HANDS BRAD A BUSINESS CARD. BRAD READS IT --

CLOSE UP: "CATERINE VAUBAN - CRUELTY, MANIPULATION,
MEANINGLESSNESS. 01133607855220"

                                        DISSOLVE TO:

EXT. MEADOW - DAY

Albert walks in a meadow, toward camera, looking past it, at
Tommy who is IN THE DISTANCE, sitting on the rock, waiting.

                    TOMMY (SHOUTS)
          HERE HE COMES.

Back to Albert still walking toward him.

                    ALBERT (WALKING)
          Oh boy.

                    TOMMY
          THE MAN POET WHO BONED FRANCE'S
          DARK LADY OF PHILOSOPHY.

Albert arrives, sits next to Tommy.

                                        (CONTINUED)

CONTINUED:

                    TOMMY (CONT'D)
THE PARKING LOT CRUSADER OF TRUTH,
WHO TURNED HIS BACK ON HIS OTHER
LIKE A COLD-BLOODED GANGSTA.

                    ALBERT
I know, I'm sorry.

                    TOMMY
But you had to do it anyway, didn't
you?

                    ALBERT
She's a powerful person, I haven't
been with a lot of women --

                    TOMMY
Obviously.

                    ALBERT
And she used me to teach us the
reality of human drama.

                    TOMMY
So is that where you get off the
ride?

                    ALBERT
Hell no.

                    TOMMY
I didn't think so. Looks like you
saw some truth.

                    ALBERT
Looks like you saw some truth.

                    TOMMY
What did you see?

                    ALBERT
The interconnection thing is
definitely real.

                    TOMMY
I know. I didn't think it was, but
it is.

                    ALBERT
And it's pretty amazing.

CONTINUED: (2)

                    TOMMY
          It is amazing. But it's also
          nothing special --

Tommy hands Albert some licorice; they bite into the licorice
as they talk.

                    ALBERT
          It grows in the manure of human
          trouble. The detectives just wanted
          to gloss over that but in fact no
          manure, no magic.

                                        CUT TO:

CATERINE, BERNARD, VIVIAN STAND TOGETHER, 60 YARDS AWAY,
WATCHING.

                    BERNARD
          Did you hear some of that?

                    VIVIAN
          Some of it sounds pretty good.

                    BERNARD
          Perhaps, I think ... maybe his case
          is closed.

                    VIVIAN
          Is it ever really closed?

                    CATERINE
          Hmmmm...

                                        BACK TO:

ALBERT AND TOMMY SIT STARING AT THE MEADOW.

                                        BACK TO:

DETECTIVES AND CATERINE STARE.

                                        BACK TO:

TOMMY AND ALBERT.

                    TOMMY (SMILES)
          What are you doing tomorrow?

                                        (CONTINUED)

CONTINUED:

> ALBERT
> I was thinking of chaining myself
> to a bulldozer. Do you want to
> come?

> TOMMY
> What time?

> ALBERT
> Like one o'clock.

> TOMMY
> That sounds good. Should I bring my
> own chains?

> ALBERT
> We always do.

They sit and stare at meadow peacefully as camera returns to
the blurry green that began the film. Fade out.

How Am I Not Myself?

Q & A

WITH DAVID O. RUSSELL
BY ROB FELD

Rob Feld: Tell me where Huckabees *came from. Were you working on something else before September 11th, perhaps, and then you started this after September 11th? Is it something of a reaction to that?*

David O. Russell: Partly. I was already working on it. I had written another script for Jason Schwartzman and decided not to make that one. I didn't feel like it was as good as I wanted it to be. *Huckabees* was sort of related to the same material. I had written a short film about fifteen years ago that I never made, but had been financed by the NEA and the New York State Council on the Arts. It was about a guy who had small microphones on all the tables of a Chinese restaurant. He would write very intense personal fortunes for everybody and then get involved with their lives. But, I ended up using that money to make *Spanking the Monkey*.

So you revived some of those ideas for Huckabees?

David: Yes, with the advantage of fifteen years' experience. Those kinds of ideas have appealed to me for a very long time. I used to go to a zendo in Manhattan very regularly, and that's what the first script that I wrote for Schwartzman was centered around. After putting that in the drawer, though, I had a dream that I was being followed by a woman detective—not for criminal reasons but for sort of spiritual ones. I thought it was really funny and would be a great launching point to talk about a lot of things that I'm into.

Would you say it was a drive to explore more personal, existential issues, or further explore the political issues you began to in **Three Kings?**

David: I think that if you're really interested in picking at the fabric of existence, you can't *not* pick at the political thread. They all make up the same fabric. During the Reagan years, I was a political organizer like Albert. After I made *Three Kings*, I knew that I didn't want to work in that huge format again, and that I wanted to return to a more human scale story that's more personal for me and about people talking to each other.

I remember you saying that **Three Kings** *was a divergence because it was very information-driven as a film.*

David: I would say *Three Kings* was information- and emotion-driven, anger-driven, and heart-broken–driven—that's what went into formulating that script for me: the information I felt everyone was denying and the emotions around that and the big lie. I couldn't believe a filmmaker hadn't picked the scab off of that first yellow ribbon war. I supported the soldiers personally, but the whole thing smacked of Reagan nostalgia as propaganda trying to conjure a monolithic World War II victory feeling, there was so much people didn't know or hadn't seen. *Huckabees* is information- and emotion-driven, too, in a different way, playing with questions that I've thought about for many years, probably beginning when I was young and read Salinger's *Franny and Zooey*, I got into the spiritual issues in that book. Then, when I went to college, I met Robert Thurman, who was then a professor at Amherst (he's now the Chairman of the Department of Religion at Columbia). He's a scholar of Indo-Tibetan studies connected with all that stuff in *Franny and Zooey*—a way of talking about these things that doesn't fall into the usual categories of religion—here are things that your mind can't really conceive of, and it's just so fantastic to begin to go into things like that. I took a bunch of courses from him. Later, I ended up going to that zendo in New York for several years. At the same time, I was still reading Bob's books, and speaking to him occasionally.

Those are the ideas that are important in the film. I've read Western philosophy, but it never rang my bell as much as Eastern philosophy, which I feel is more succinct and accessible about a lot of the same questions. One of my favorite Zen teachers is Nyogen Senzaki, a guy who died in Los Angeles in 1958, and didn't even think he should have a temple. Again, outside the usual parameters of what we expect in this area, so it's going to avoid

a lot of things that could make it feel pushy or dogmatic or cultish to someone like me. Senzaki was a highly revered Zen master who emigrated from
Japan, became a waiter, and just taught out of his apartment in downtown
LA. His book, which some lady did with him in the '50s, is like five pages
long, compared with some tome by Kant. To me, it hits a lot of the same
ideas without tying yourself up in knots, which I feel Western philosophers
tend to do.

**You mentioned Thurman's humor. Tell me a story from your time with
him.**

David: He's just a loose and funny guy with a towering intellect and
years of disciplined scholarship in many different languages, but he talks real
loose and grins a lot, with his glass eye looking off to one side. When he's
talking about esoteric concepts or ancient texts he talks about them with
intense authority yet also with humor. The texts themselves are funny, and
he relishes the humor in these old sutras. In the Vimilikirti sutra there's a part
where Sariputra is debating a higher god about the nature of form, and the
god turns Sariputra into a woman to show him how malleable forms are.
When Bob reads this out loud he always turns Sariputra's voice into a hap-
less falsetto that's funny. Then there's the part where the adepts and bod-
hisattvas have to send out for chairs so they can all sit in Vimilikirti's house,
and they debate which galaxy the best chairs come from. They get these
massive chairs that are miles high yet paradoxically fit into this little house,
again exploding all ideas of time and space, and powdering poor Sariputra,
who's no slouch, by the way. That's what's hilarious about the sutra and about
Bob; it repeatedly shows how no one person can conceive of the vastness of
the truth of reality, and there's no end to unpacking it. If this isn't getting
across Bob's humor, then I guess you had to be there.

Three Kings *had a very hard-won and original look and quality. With
the theme of "open spaces" in* **Huckabees,** *tell me how you approached the
aesthetic for* **Huckabees.**

David: The exteriors were chosen to look like strip mall land, which
could be anywhere in America, especially when there's some extant piece of
greenery boxed in by road and houses and development. The interiors were
specifically made to be uncluttered, clean, and the palette was to include no
red (with very few exceptions), and no green except for the trees. And no

blue jeans because it was a formal world of people who are serious about these things; they're not to be confused with any new-age stuff that feels casual or without discipline and rigor. Thurman was never the Nehru guy. He was the rumpled Oxford shirt with the suit. I was creating a new context for these ideas—a secular, unfamiliar context, a bit European, because the detectives and their nemesis studied together in Paris, another world where ideas are considered as a culture. Antonioni's *Blow-Up*—the clean '60s feeling was an inspiration. And Bunuel's *Discreet Charm of the Bourgeoisie*. It's beautiful to me when some frames are almost black and white because everything is within one palette range. Light blue, yellow, orange, navy, black, these were the colors, primarily.

I know you worked with Lily Tomlin before, in* Flirting with Disaster. *Tell me a bit about the process of constructing this cast.

David: Dustin had me come to his house and read the script to him out loud, over a period of several days. He wanted to hear it the way I heard it. We would stop and discuss lots of different things. He was very concerned it wouldn't be accessible to a wide audience and that it would be an art film. I told him it was an art film first and foremost; if it has a wider life, it will come from that. He said, "Okay, then it's fine." I gave him Bob Thurman's lectures on audio and video.

Lily and I have been friends since *Flirting with Disaster* and I fought to keep her in the cast when studios would throw younger, bigger names at me. That happened briefly with Dustin's part as well—they always try to get you to cast younger people. Lily was busy doing her show, so we didn't get to hang out that much beforehand, but she gets a lot of this intuitively.

Jason and I had been spending time together since I saw *Rushmore* and wrote that first script for him, which got put in a drawer. He went and spent time with activists like Chad Griffin, who was fighting to save a huge tract of land in the Santa Monica mountains. Jason gave himself to soaking up everything he could to become this character.

Mark and I have been fairly close friends since *Three Kings*, and he listened to Thurman as well. We had lots of talks about the character being fierce and vulnerable at the same time, which Mark absolutely has in him. We also meditated and prayed a few times, which is nothing strange to Mark because he prays quite a lot.

Jude and I had been speaking for a few years about trying to do something. He's one of the least insecure actors I have ever met and a very inquisitive guy, who is willing to dive into anything, and got off on deconstructing the golden movie star in his character. His life was undergoing a deconstruction at the time, a lot of upheaval, and he was glad to get out of London and put this energy into his character. The fact that he and Naomi are primarily dramatic actors was perfect because, first off, it was fun for them to be kind of crazy and funny. Second, they bring a lot of reality to their parts, and the comedy would have to come from that, but I knew they both liked to play and laugh.

Naomi played ping-pong and goofed around the first time she came over to talk, and Jude is very easy to play with, while also being quite serious about the work. Naomi was concerned that she would not be funny because she had been told in the past that she wasn't. I kept assuring her she would be funny and that she is funny because . . . she's funny. She had just come from *21 Grams* and she still had a lot of crying that would just come out of her at different moments, and then be gone. That was perfect for the character of Dawn, who is split between her old self and something else. Fragile. It was also fun for her to put on those colorful sexy outfits.

Caterine was first intended for Catherine Deneuve—but we were fortunate to get Huppert instead because Huppert makes a much better match with Jason—she brings her own dark gravity and she's extremely sexy and lithe. If you get past her tough exterior, she is very playful and sweet.

My mother-in-law plays a small role that she actually played in real life—a tough town-council member—and she plays it effortlessly. When my wife would hear her saying lines in the house she would cringe at a particular caustic tone that was familiar.

I was also so glad that Talia Shire was willing to play her own son's mother—though that's not who she is at all, that character. It took some cajoling because she was very conscious of not wanting to crash Jason's party, but he didn't care, he was happy to have her.

How much did you allow them to improvise?
David: Ideas always come up. We're always trying to make it better.

During the audio commentary on **Three Kings**, *you talked about how influential the time you spent in Central America was on you and your view of* **Three Kings.** *I can't help but relate your political point-of-view between* *the two films, so can you tell me a bit about the time you spent there, and what you took away with you?*

David: I had taken time off from college, spent time with some exiles from Chile, and then back at college, wrote all about the American-backed coup that put a dictator there, and how full of shit that was, how wrong, how infuriating. Then there was Nicaragua and they overthrew the scumbag dictator, which was exhilarating. I wanted to go down there. I had worked in the States to send stuff to the Sandinistas, like eyeglasses and money, so I got a letter of introduction to them so they would know I wasn't working for the CIA. And then I got down there and of course it's nothing like you pictured.

I worked for the literacy campaign out in the sticks. The Third World itself was just so different and so poor and so hard to live in, that alone kind of saps a lot of your energy. The Sandinistas were real Cuban/Russian-influenced and rigidly doctrinaire, which of course was ultimately a disappointment. But I got to be in the middle of a huge social upheaval as it was happening, and so many people were so filled with hope and energy and questions.

Me and a Nicaraguan friend would get up with a guitar in front of hundreds of farmers at these rallies and sing Beatles and Woody Guthrie songs— and we weren't very good at all, but everyone would be so eager for more because they didn't have TVs or stereos or anything; we were the only entertainment that night.

It was exciting and fun in many ways, and also heartbreaking, because things didn't get to change as much as people wanted. I wish the U.S. didn't come down on them with the Contra war because it just sapped an already poor, beat-down country even further, instead of letting them find some sort of social-democratic solution with free enterprise, with some planning and some help, for God's sake, from the superpower that had backed Somoza for so long.

So from all of this, I could relate to the Iraqis I met who rose up against Saddam in '91 and got crushed. And I had a kind of natural sense for what Third World–living feels and looks like, with the exposed rebar and half-completed buildings and the occasional new car rolling past the worst kind of shantytowns and the top 40 hits that are already outdated in the U.S. but are new down there. Simply being in a country that has lived for decades with an American-supported dictator, you learn a lot from that. And I suppose it galvanizes anyone working to change things, I came back from Nicaragua with no shame about standing in a parking lot handing out fliers to fight toxic waste or whatever, with teenage pricks throwing garbage at me—and this informs the Albert character in *Huckabees*. I might make a movie about my experience down there some day: Schwartzman in Managua.

*You know, as I was watching **Huckabees**, I thought a lot about Charlie Kaufman and Wes Anderson. They both use semi fringe or exaggerated characters to approach kind of existential issues, also with a great absurdist humor. Do you relate to those guys at all, to their films?*

David: Albert may be fringe but he's not exaggerated for me—he is me from when I was in my early twenties, and a lot of the Mark Wahlberg character, too. I had very intense political or philosophical confrontations with people all the time because I took those things very seriously and they were my life. As for *Rushmore*, it had a very big impact on me because I obviously related to that character. He's very committed, not philosophically or politically, but in other ways I related to—I mean, I organized a kids committee to campaign for Humphrey against Nixon when I was ten years old, and let me tell you that when Nixon won I was devastated and questioned the nature of humanity. In high school, I started an alternative newspaper that was at the center of several scandals where we were summoned to the principal's house (this was a large public high school) at like eleven at night and he was trying to stop us from distributing the paper the next day, which was exciting at the time, and reminds me of the culture of making a movie, the stakes and the intensity. So on *Three Kings*, I would sit in my trailer watching *Rushmore* and wishing I was living in Rushmore because it was so much more appealing than the desert of soldiers outside the trailer. That's how I fell in love with Jason Schwartzman. As for Charlie Kaufman and Spike, the films they've made together, I find them inspiring and brilliant, even if it's a sensibility that is darker or more anguished than what I'm personally drawn to.

Do you think it has become difficult to be earnest in a film? Are audiences expecting a degree of cynicism and irony, and do they distrust "the straight story"? Pre-9/11 many filmmakers would tell me that's how they felt but I really haven't asked the question since.

David: I think so. The sound-bite media culture is geared toward mocking and quick judgments and negativity. "Ooh, snap!" What is especially difficult for audiences I think is if you're being *somewhat* ironic, but not completely ironic; or being somewhat earnest while also finding the humor in the characters, still being able to step back from them, but not necessarily crushing them. There were some people, not a lot, but some, who saw *Huckabees* and said, "Mark's character is such a loser and Jason's character is such a loser and the detectives are ineffective and a joke" and I thought, What are you talking about? These guys aren't losers, I love these people, I believe in them. Just because they're different or failing or laughable doesn't relegate them to the "loser" category. That's such an oppressive polarity to live by, it eliminates so many shades in between.

Talk to me about the two warring philosophies in **Huckabees.** *There's the more Eastern perspective, that everything is connected, as espoused by the existential detectives, Bernard and Vivian Jaffe [Dustin Hoffman and Lily Tomlin], and the more Western-influenced Caterine Vauban [Isabelle Huppert], for whom nothing matters.*

David: Hoffman and Tomlin are more informed by Thurman, and go into more Indo-Tibetan ideas, whereas Isabelle Huppert is sort of a cocktail of Sartre and Zen and nihilism. Zen has a much more blunt, undecorated approach than some Indo-Tibetan literature. It's more like, "What is it right *now?* What's happening *now?*" There's no deities, no visions, none of that. It's just, What it is right *now?* And if it's joyful, be it, and if it's painful, then be it, don't discriminate. And I like that about her. She has something to offer. I think Sartre approached that a little bit, too, when he talks about his nausea, realizing that every construction that holds us up—cultural, political, physical—is sort of a tissue paper. And that, ultimately, there's really nothing holding us at all. I think he takes it a little too far—as does the Isabelle Huppert character. They say there's nothing holding us, period, whereas the detectives say everything is less solid than we assume, but everything is held by everything else —a less nihilistic view. Sartre and the Huppert character are responding to the old views that we're held in some net of religion and culture—which has its roots in the dogma of the middle ages when they burned people for daring to think beyond that, including scientists, which is why science is still dogmatically opposed to considering matters of consciousness or the soul, even though they're not going to be burned at the stake today. When I read Sartre's life history, it's obvious to me that his childhood colored the bleakness of his philosophy, as did his war experience. And that kind of meant two things to me. It meant, Well, how could you say that is the truth of existence, just because it was a truth of *your* past? How can you make an absolute out of it? But, at the same time, he could say, "You know what? This happened to me, so why isn't it reality?" Just like when Vauban takes Albert to his parents' house and says, "Yeah, this shit happens, what about that? Why is that any less real than some more advanced idea of consciousness?" Sometimes it's liberating to accept the disappointment that fills this world, but then, do you make an entire consciousness of that? A world view? Vauban is kind of stuck in the backwater of resentment and darkness.

Is it easier to focus on that stuff, as opposed to the opposite extremes of joy and the happiness?

David: Is it easier to go dark? I think so. I think that's what makes this movie more vulnerable because it's not just taking the dark position, it's out there with the Hoffman and Tomlin characters and their affirmative vision. It's not making these guys out to be jokers. It's saying, I take them seriously. I think it's a lot easier in cinema—especially independent cinema—to talk about how fucked up everything is or to give you a fucked-up experience (which is often a cliché in its own way) without availing yourself of some sort of joy or some of these other windows into a larger frame of mind.

A lot of what you do has a great deal of humor in it, and you use it to talk about issues that are difficult to approach.

David: I think it's not good to take anything too seriously, although I have done this repeatedly throughout my life, which then leads me to laugh at myself. I think that truth is full of humor because it's filled with contradictions and other things that pull the rug out from under us, and that's good. You have to be willing to look foolish. What they'll tell you all the time in Zen is to be willing to be a fool. And these characters are my favorite kind of people: They're willing to appear foolish. When they focus on something that they think is true, or revealing of the truth, they're not going to let it go. They're not going to go back to business as usual. They're going to stay with it, regardless of what social conventions it completely messes up in their lives, like a marriage, job, or friendships. And that's what I love about Tommy, the Mark Wahlberg character. That's what I love about all these characters.

It's not quite a moment of nirvana that's achieved, is it?

David: They say you know you're on the path of truth when you see a big pile of shit, not flowers and cupcakes. Albert and Tommy are guys who have latched on to a line of inquiry, and they're serious about it. And I think there's a kind of nirvana in that tenacious plunge, but it's mixed up with all the shit. And in the meantime, it looks funny to us some of the time as they pursue this inquiry.

They found the right question?

David: Well, a *good* question, anyway. You've got to live the questions, as Rilke said.

Tommy reflects a lot of the questions I asked after 9/11, about the petroleum thing. Everything he says, I agree with. If we had stopped using petroleum in the late '70s, as we were starting to, there would never have been a first Gulf War. We would never have remained complicit with these dictatorships, which are spawning terrorism, for the sake of oil. And we would have had the moral high ground, in terms of trying to promote democracy in that area, instead of just trying to get oil. And then we say, "Well, we supported this dictator but now we don't support him because we think he's mean. But before we supported him because we needed the oil and we didn't like Iran." You know, that just blows my mind. It's like all the people saying when Reagan died, "Reagan: the right man at the right time." What the fuck are you talking about? I don't understand how every journalist in the country could start saying that. It's like some kind of collective sleep, or something. Ronald Reagan was no joke: he was the beginning of something very bad that's still going on. As for Schwartzy's character, Albert loves the open spaces and sees that they're getting closed in. This is also a pet peeve of mine. I think that *Spanking the Monkey* was probably the only claustrophobic movie I've made because there's the claustrophobic world of that home. I like very open spaces, like the desert in *Three Kings* or the open road in *Flirting with Disaster* or the rooms of this movie. They're very open. But you can see Albert's is a losing game, as Vauban said. We're going to develop everything to within an inch of its life, and you won't know what happens in the meadow at dusk anymore. "What happens in the meadow at dusk? Everything, nothing. Everything, nothing. Everything, nothing."

While doing the film, did you find an answer for yourself to "Why does my work matter?"

David: I will say that it was really fun making a movie about things that interest me a great deal. My job continued my inquiry and my learning about these things. But this can always be the case if you're paying attention, I guess.

In many of your films you use a brand of absurd humor, and I'm wondering what that means to you? Is absurdity our/your experience of the world?

David: I don't know what to say except that it's my taste in comedy. Serious things are funny. The detectives can be funny while they ask you, "What about infinity?" right now while you're at work. Lily's character is going to talk to you about what you had for breakfast and what's happening with your job, and what's happening with your relationships. She's going to be very specific down at the micro level while Dustin's all macro. And, of course, they're the same thing. I thought, how wonderful to catch somebody out of the corner of your eye, in the middle of your banal tension, and remember, "Oh, yeah, that infinity thing." That totally flips your mind upside down.

And suddenly you see the relationship between the infinity thing and the—

David: Well, maybe you don't, but it's certainly going to snap your mind out of how seriously it's taking some conflict or situation. It's going to put it in a larger context, maybe loosen your grip and open you up a little bit. You're not going to get an answer right away. But you start to have a different experience maybe.

Did you model each of these characters on a specific writer?

David: Bob Thurman is Dustin a little bit. Lily is probably some amalgamation of shrinks and scientists I've known, people who are very specific and rigorous. And Isabelle, like I said, is probably just some version of Sartre or Simone de Beauvoir plus Zen monks I've known. The whole world of Paris in the '50s tickles me. A subculture that lives and dies on ideas and experiences derived from them.

I think we're having some minor moments of that as a reaction to George W. Bush now. But after these moments, does everyone just go back to complacence and indifference? In Huckabees, *Albert is orphaned by indifference, and Tommy asks, "How come people only ask these questions when something really bad happens?" What's the importance, to you, of asking these questions all the time?*

David: That was true about 9/11. There were actually about two months during which people asked, "Wow, what is our society? What is our culture? What is my existence?" Then it was, "Aaaaand cut!" Let's get back to business as usual, and just talk about the evil terrorists.

What must this feel like to you, with us back in Iraq after making Three Kings, *which was something of an impassioned plea?*

David: Yeah, it was, in a way. I mostly thought it was very ironic that we had gone right to the doorstep of Baghdad, with this intricately composed international coalition, but then said, "Okay, he's out of Kuwait and he's crushing his people again, but we gotta go." I don't know. I'm not saying it would be easy to get rid of him or to take over Iraq, but it just seemed unbelievably ironic to me, like some horrible riddle, that we would go to the edge, protect our oil, and leave the dictator there. I thought it pointed to our real intentions in the Gulf. What bothers me about Bush is that he went back to get rid of Saddam, but he hasn't asked one question about energy policy or what we're really in the Gulf for: to get oil, which causes so many problems.

Or, he just says, "Well, we need to get out of here so let's drill in ANWR [Alaska's Arctic National Wildlife Refuge]," which doesn't wean us from oil, or even foreign oil, so much as present a momentary quick fix.

David: The politician as the indulgent parent. "I'll only tell you what you want to hear and what's easy for you." That's what happened with Reagan, because people felt "Carter's making me think about stuff. I don't like that. Ronald Reagan told me everything was okay. I like that better. I can just drive my car and I don't have to worry about anything. Malaise?

What's a malaise? I don't want to think about that! Shut up, Jimmy Carter!" And the media is hand in glove with this stuff because it's like a studio trying to sell movies or Budweiser trying to sell beer. They're slaves to lazy popular opinion. They'll be the first ones to tell you that people loved Reagan and don't want to ask those questions. Show me a politician who's brave enough to say to people, "Listen, I'm going to give you a choice here. I think we should get off of foreign oil, and oil in general, for XYZ reasons—the environment not being the least of them, but there's plenty of other reasons—like we're complicit with these dictatorships and it's going to bite us on the ass. Let's take a vote, and if you guys say 'No,' then fine, you've made the choice to not think about this stuff, but you're going to live with the consequences." Clinton did a lot of good stuff—appointing judges, protecting land—but he never even talked about this. I mean, once he got bitchslapped on health care, he got very careful (except with his cock).

It was health care and gays in the military—
David: Yeah. He didn't really take a lot of other bold positions after that, like saying to the American people, "Let's talk about oil for a second." And even with Al Gore as vice president. Our political discourse and media increasingly become about lazy sound bites. The journalists I talk to tell me that they're increasingly unable to ask questions and be more reflective because their stories have to be shorter and shorter. If you look at anything from *Newsweek* to *Blender*, it's just little bites of information, which at their best could be like haiku. But since most people aren't up to the demands of a haiku—something that's going to be short and paradoxical and inquiring—it's probably going to end up being oversimplified. It ends up like the McLaughlin Group: "The situation in Iraq? Too slow! Next guy. Too slow! I hate Arabs! Right! Next answer..." Try saying that George Bush violated the Constitution and you get, "What? That sounds complicated and political." Say Monica gave Bill Clinton a blow job, and it's, "That's a story I can understand." So the media panders to the smallest mind of the public, as do Republicans. And it's kind of a spiral.

Yeah. I was at the Democratic National Conventions last week, which was only given so much press coverage, but you should have seen them chasing Ben Affleck.
David: Shiny objects, like jingling your keys in front of a crying baby.

News feels largely like entertainment at this point, doesn't it? I mean, that line between journalism and entertainment gets blurred more every day, and I feel like the incarnation we're experiencing now began with the first Gulf War, when CNN started with the graphics and theme music. Now who can tell the difference between the news and **Entertainment Tonight?**

David: You should see the morning shows out here in LA, where the girls practically wear bikinis. The most popular morning show has this guy, who's like 55 or 60, with these two super hot girls. I remember seeing it after the Bush/Gore election, and I was like, Well, that's why Bush won. Just look at this morning show and it tells you everything you need to know about why Bush won. It's all in the little tops and the giggles and the subtext is "No thinking or questioning." People used to think our totalitarian future would look like Orwell's *1984* or Bradbury's *Fahrenheit 411* with an oppressive police state—but the mind-control turned out to be more insidious than that—it looks like "Wild on E."

Where did **Huckabees** *begin? Did it start out being about this stuff?*

David: It went through many permutations, and there were some versions that were like three-hundred pages long, because I write every fun arc that I want, with every character, and Jeff and I did a lot of that. Then, once you've got all this material, you can say, Okay, now how can this work in a compact way? We worked on it and worked on it, and it's ambitious material to take on in a comedic way, and it felt impossible to nail it perfectly, which coincidentally is what Bob or other teachers will say about truth. So I knew that it was a bit like jumping off a cliff to make this movie, and part of it was me saying, "I don't care. This interests me enough, and it's fun enough, we've worked it out enough, so let's just say 'Geronimo' and jump into it and hope it's fun."

Was it more of that than you've done in the past?

David: Totally. But also, what I think makes the movie a little bit more vulnerable is that the ideas are not wrapped up in a war movie or an action movie, *The Matrix*. Questions like these are usually wrapped in a sci-fi movie. But, in *Huckabees*, it's just a comedy about people who ask these questions, period. It's not like these people have some other incarnation as a sci-fi hero.

The very nature and essence of these people is to ask these questions.

David: Yeah. So, it's a more direct approach, which I think makes it more …

Something of a tightrope walk? I mean, you could lose people.

David: Exactly. In other words, it's probably easier to get people if it's a sci-fi movie, or wrapped up in some story that is something other than overtly these questions.

Well, I found it legitimately funny, and that's never a bad way to present material.

David: That's great because the intention is to have fun with the picture.

The plot revolves around Albert's coincidences, but there were some coincidences surrounding this film.

David: I have had some strange coincidences in my life that made me wonder. Here's one that happened in pre-production: Derek Jeter, who was a celebrity referred to in the script as a Huckabees endorser like Pete Sampras, was seriously injured with a dislocated shoulder in the Yankees home opener when he had a collision with the Toronto catcher named…Ken Huckaby.

After making **Three Kings,** *and now with us back in Iraq, how do we live with our losing battles?*

David: Oh, you just made me think of something. The conscience. Impossible causes, which is very Quixotic, literally. Don Quixote, taking on an impossible cause. In a way, that's sort of an existential conundrum. How can you work on something when it seems like it's just a drop in the bucket? At the beginning of the movie, Albert has a litany of cussing in his head, which you can have when you're so frustrated with the inability to affect anything, to a perverse extent. I thought 9/11 was filled with perversity; the perversity of great grief and sorrow, yet maintaining an unwillingness to examine certain things. To me, that's kind of perverse. It's like, what does it take? If we're not going to do it now, we're not going to think about our energy policy now, I don't think we ever are. But, by the end of the movie, Albert is able to sit there and sort of embrace this dark human truth a little more. At least he's not cussing. He's moved an inch, but it's a very critical inch. He's on the same rock, just as frustrated as before, but he sort of accepts the bargain. There's something absurd and paradoxical about that. I accept this bargain that seems endless and to not have a lot of traction, and that doesn't always have the impact that I want, but I'm not going to walk away from it and just go do whippits all day. I'm going to keep doing it.

Rob Feld interviewed David O. Russell by telephone and e-mail August-September 2004. Feld began his life in New York film and theater working under legendary director Wynn Handman at the American Place Theater. Feld later worked at Vanguard Films, under producer John Williams, on such films as *Seven Years in Tibet* and *Shrek*. Feld began freelancing in New York's indie film scene, eventually partnering at the New York- and London-based media and film production company ManifestoVision. Feld has written screenplays for production companies such as Vanguard, and his interviews with noted filmmakers are published regularly in such journals as the Writers and Directors Guild of America's magazines, *Written By* and *DGA Magazine*.

PRODUCTION NOTES

At the center of *I ♥ Huckabees* lies Albert Markovski, whose curiosity about a niggling coincidence sparks him to hire Existential Detectives who will stop at nothing to examine the very contours of his existence. An earnest and devoted environmentalist fighting to preserve dwindling open spaces, Albert Markovski has reached a crossroads he hopes the detectives can see him through: should he continue fighting for his dream of wild marshes or give them up entirely and start all over?

The character holds a place near to director David O. Russell's own heart. "I have been, in my day, an organizer for a cause or two, and I have been in parking lots talking to people and handing out fliers, and I've had people mock me for it, but I didn't care," admits Russell. "These characters are my favorite kind of people—searchers who will not let business as usual get in their way of experiencing or finding the truth."

Most of all, Albert dares to tackle questions that a lot of people relegate to midnight sweats. Russell continues: "Albert isn't fooling around when it comes to asking, What is this experience we're having? How can we make sense of the world? Are things hopeless or is there the possibility for hope? He's passionate about these questions, which is what I like about the character. But like most people in investigations, he's also hiding crucial information from himself, information he isn't prepared to deal with—principally, his humiliating relationship with Brad Stand."

Albert Markovski's wild journey really kicks off once the Existential Detectives, Bernard and Vivian Jaffe, decide to take on his complicated case. To play these metaphysical private eyes, David O. Russell was thrilled to be able to cast two cinematic icons: Dustin Hoffman and Lily Tomlin.

"They're both intense people—very smart and interested in politics and ideas, with huge hearts—and they play these roles very real, which is exactly what I was looking for in the film; a kind of comedy that is fun, but also real and committed. They both possess an incredible intuition and were able to constantly find the balance and know when to cross the line into broader humor," says Russell. "I think they make a great couple. They feel like real academics to me, eccentric but not silly; confident and formal, but also passionate."

For Dustin Hoffman the role of Bernard was a welcome departure from anything else he'd ever done—or encountered—in his diverse career. "To put it simply, I've never played an Existential Detective before, so that's what attracted to me the part," he says. To aid Hoffman in diving further into the philosophical foundations that underlie the role, David O. Russell sent him videotaped lectures of Robert Thurman, a renowned scholar and Professor of Indo-Tibetan Studies at Columbia University.

In answer to the question "What is *I ♥ Huckabees* about?" Hoffman says: "I think it was Marcel Duchamp who said that it's wrong to define art by name. Art is meaning. In twentieth-century painting, he went on to say, art became conceptual. He believed that it was not just retinal, visual. It goes to our brain matter. In fact, he said art is really about defining what art is. It's what art means rather than just giving it a name.

"So I think David O. Russell is trying to get past what life is on a literal level in order to get to what life means."

Hoffman continues: "The film is there to provoke feelings from you. Perhaps even to provoke you to ask the question that you have asked me to answer."

Another draw for Hoffman was the chance to work with Lily Tomlin. "I had never worked with Lily before," he says. "I had simply admired her from a distance. I always felt she was much more than a comedian. I believe she is a character actor and, in fact, an artist. Working with her was simply a gift that was given to me, and I thank her for it."

Tomlin had a blast with the script for *I ♥ Huckabees*, which she happily notes defies even the most rigorous attempts at categorization. "In some ways, it's a classic farce but it also deals with the wacky human condition," she summarizes. "It's about so, so many things — but for me, it's all the layers that David O. Russell has created...that's really the delight of it."

Tomlin was especially drawn in by the notion of the two Existential Detectives who comb through their client's hidden lives looking for nebulous clues. "Bernard and Vivian are so comedic to me," she says. "They're sort of like intellectuals who have gotten out of control! I particularly enjoy how they battle with Caterine over the best way to fix the world and fix their clients' lives—and how they each try to prove that their way is the best way, the right one, the correct one, and yet they can't seem to do without one another. There's a wonderful yin and yang to that."

In the role of Vivian, Tomlin also had a chance to be a witness to a rarely seen side of Oscar®-winning actor Dustin Hoffman. "I expected Dustin to be very pensive, very savvy, a terribly serious artist, you know? But in the role of Bernard, he was so much fun—always very on, and so sweet and so playful. We had a tremendous amount of fun together."

The actor Russell always had in mind to embody Markovski was Jason Schwartzman, who came to the fore in Wes Anderson's *Rushmore*. "From the minute I saw *Rushmore*, I was in love with Jason and wanted to work with him," says Russell. "We got to know each other over the years, and I got to like him even more. We have a lot in common. I wrote one movie for him, then decided it wasn't ready. Then I wrote this script and Markovski was meant for him."

When Jason Schwartzman read *I* ♥ *Huckabees*, he found the very notion of detectives who might prowl through your transient thoughts and emotions instead of your closets highly intriguing. From the minute he read the script, he wondered to himself: "Would I ever go to an Existential Detective?" Like Albert Markovski, he decided it might not be such a bad idea.

"I began to think about how sometimes we all get so far into our heads that we forget which way is up and which way is down, and at those points it would indeed be nice to have somebody to remind you of who and where you are," says Schwartzman. "I think most of us have that already to a certain degree. We all have people who in times of desperation and confusion come to our aid and help us make sense of things. They're really just like Existential Detectives—except they don't get paid for it."

Drawn to the film's unconventional premise, Schwartzman was also drawn to Albert's unexpected serio-comic journey which takes him to a place rarely visited in films: the edges of human consciousness. "I think we all know someone like Albert," notes Schwartzman. "He's an environmentalist, a nice guy and a poet, although not necessarily in that order. Then quite suddenly he's thrust into this investigation to find the meaning of his life, to piece together all the shards of his existence and try to make some kind of sense out of the chaos. What I liked most about him is that this guy really, fervently, wants to know what's going on, not just with himself, but with the universe and beyond the universe. That's an interesting position to be in."

Schwartzman was also thrilled to work with such a diverse and award-winning cast, especially the two actors who join him as the Existential Detective's clients: Jude Law as the impeccable Brad Stand and Mark Wahlberg as the fiercely big-hearted Tommy Corn. "These are wonderful actors," notes Schwartzman. "And now I can get reservations for any restaurant anywhere. I just say I know Mark Wahlberg, and I get in."

Albert Markovski, and his snowballing search for answers, is joined by firefighter Tommy Corn, whose ever-deepening post-9/11 concerns about the world's petroleum dependency have caused him to also come to the Existential Detectives for aid. David O. Russell explains, "Tommy is someone who's not willing to go on the way everyone else is in the face of some horrible contradictions. He is someone who looked at 9/11, in which he lost some of his firefighter brothers, and asked 'Why did this happen?' 'Why do we participate with oil dictatorships in the Middle East?' He wants to know whether this stuff really matters—because if it does then we're acting very stupidly about it—and if it doesn't, then does that mean anything goes and everything is meaningless? These are big questions he's sitting with, but of course there's also comedy in this because his search is painful, unresolved and absurd, just like life. And there's also comedy in the way life brings him around to feeling some mysterious connection and hope."

Russell wrote the part of Tommy for Mark Wahlberg, with whom he first collaborated for *Three Kings*. "I think Mark is this character in certain ways," he says. "He's unflinching in the way he perceives things and the world breaks his heart, yet he's very tough and defensive about it. He's a tough guy for real—and it's a beautiful thing to get him to be so vulnerable and put it all out there. In his performance, you get toughness in the service of vulnerability, an unusual combination of scary intensity combined with human caring and concern."

Wahlberg couldn't wait to work with Russell after his first experience. "We have a relationship that is totally honest and unlike any I've had with any other filmmaker," he comments. "This is a very special relationship. I have complete trust in David and his vision. And this was also an irresistible situation, to work with Jason, Dustin, Lily, Jude, Naomi and Isabelle. When you work with people like that, it can only elevate your game."

Nevertheless, the film took Wahlberg on a wild ride through his own riled-up questions and emotions, as he took on Tommy. "I think I've been pushed harder on this film than I ever have before," he says. "I went a lot more out on a limb with this character and did a lot of hard work. David asked me to do a lot of preparing. He gave me lots of stuff to read and watch and to listen to, and a lot of counsel. He spent hours interviewing me about my thoughts on life and love. I even went to see a therapist."

Ultimately, Wahlberg recognizes similarities between himself and Tommy. "I can probably be as extreme as Tommy on certain issues, but it's just not the same issues," he says. "We all have things we focus a lot of energy into, things that drive us so crazy we can't see straight. He's a challenging character, but those are the best kind."

Another character who poses a challenge to both Albert Markovski and the Existential Detectives is Jude Law's Brad Stand, the quintessentially upwardly mobile young man with a perpetual tan and blinding grin. While climbing the corporate ladder at Huckabees, Brad has never had a second thought about the costs of his ever-accelerating life . . . until now.

Like everyone else in the cast, Law spent his own restless nights wondering about the film's story. "It's a story that's filled with all kinds of themes, potential messages and filmic conceits," he observes. "But I think it's ultimately about those questions that everyone asks themselves: am I really happy?...How can I make myself really happy?"

For Law, these questions were key to playing Brad Stand, who is forced against his far more superficial instincts to dive deeper and deeper into his well-hidden anxieties and fears during the course of the film. "I think Brad is the character in the film who has the most layers to unravel," he explains. "Brad is so firmly entrenched in the personality he puts forward to the world that he's basically stopped asking himself: 'Who am I and what makes me tick?' He's all about pleasing people, but only in the most political and fake way. So, when he starts to unravel, he has a lot of interesting revelations."

Part of Law's challenge was also to humanize Brad. "I think there are parts of each of the characters in this film in everyone. And when it comes to Brad, we all have some of his qualities," he says. "I'm as guilty as anyone of sometimes putting on a phony face or putting on a pretense so I don't ever have to question the world or my existence. I want to please people, as well. Don't we all?"

David O. Russell says of Law's performance, "Jude has a golden quality, an ability to be almost too gorgeous and likable and human. As an actor, he is fearless and fun and willing to investigate what is in front of him with body and soul. He managed to play the role without making it in any way a cartoon. His character is the toughest nut to crack. Everybody else kind of gets penetrated and busted down in the course of the movie, but Brad hangs on."

Brad's shimmering world of success first starts to crash at his feet when he tries to take over Albert Markovski's Open Spaces Coalition. In the ensuing conflict with Albert, Brad comes face to face with a conflicted soul he was previously unaware of even having. Law notes that the intense production brought him and Jason Schwartzman, like their characters, closer. "Jason and I pretty much went through everything that Albert and Brad go through together," he says. "We found ourselves fighting and arguing, having probably the most heartfelt fun on camera that I have ever had."

Law continues: "In a sense, I feel like I have gone to the Existential Detectives in making this film. None of us could have played these parts without asking some of these questions of ourselves. But of course, they're still there, and if Lily Tomlin and Dustin Hoffman really were Existential Detectives, I think I would make an appointment."

Then there is Brad's girlfriend Dawn, the Barbie-blonde spokesmodel for Huckabees, who puts a hitch in his plans when she makes some radical changes in her own life and appearance. "Brad's relationship with Dawn is fascinating because it's the shallowest kind of emotional bond that's all about both of them relying on one another to reinforce who the other person is," says Jude Law. "She's very beautiful and successful, and he's never considered what would happen without those things."

Playing Dawn is versatile, award-winning actress Naomi Watts in an unusual comic turn that drops facades – literally. "Working with Naomi was absolutely terrific," notes Law. "We both came to the set ready to dive into this head first. We had a lot of fun breaking through Brad and Dawn's tough skins, and she was a great ally."

David O. Russell cast Watts because in her he found "a very smart, amazingly talented blonde who could play a dumb blonde with enough honest sincerity and commitment that we believe that she might suddenly transform herself," he explains. Russell continues: "Naomi Watts has amazing skills and focus, along with a deep willingness to try anything. She was the perfect person to deconstruct a golden American ideal."

Watts was immediately attracted to the role of Dawn. "I love to play women who are on the verge of something, and that certainly describes Dawn," the actress notes. "I really enjoyed her because she makes this huge and unexpected transformation. I mean, shallow as she is, she has a certain self-awareness that things are not how they should be and she starts reaching for more. It's really what all the characters in the film do in one way or another – each realizing there's so much more to discover."

But Dawn's metamorphosis is perhaps the most dramatic in the film, necessitating that Watts literally strip herself bare as the story progresses. "I was a little nervous about it but I also thought that it would be incredibly fun to play this gooey, glossy, Barbie Doll-blonde becoming totally unhinged, hitting rock bottom and then finding peace," says Watts. "It's a serious journey but it's also comic, which is something I haven't really done before. And that's one of the things that's so wonderful about David O. Russell. He makes films because he wants you to think—and there are some very cerebral things going on in this movie but he makes them visceral through humor."

Watts first met her on-screen partner Jude Law on the set of I ❤ Huckabees. "David O. Russell wanted us to be in character right from the very beginning. On the first day, I walked into the room with Jude, and David immediately said, 'Now, go sit in his lap.' So that was our introduction! But we had a wonderful time working together," recalls Watts. "He's such an extraordinary actor that he can actually make you forget that he's one of the most beautiful men in the world. He embodied the soul of his character so deeply, that all I saw was Brad Stand."

Completing the existential circle that surrounds Albert, Brad, Tommy and Dawn is acclaimed French actress Isabelle Huppert in the role of Caterine Vauban, the philosophical enemy of the Existential Detectives. Says David O. Russell of the rivalry between them: "Caterine expresses a feeling everyone has but is so frightening, we usually have to suppress it—that there's a lot about life that just plain sucks and is a lousy deal. Caterine sees life as an oscillation between the cruel and absurd theater of human drama and suffering on the one hand, and, on the other, the peace attained from just being and not thinking, which takes a lot of practice, which is part of what sucks, that peace takes practice. But the Existential Detectives take it further and say, there's some magic here, that there's a huge mystery beyond our comprehension that we're interwoven into. Of course, I'm with Caterine on plenty of days, and I'm with the Detectives on other days.

They're both equally important."

As for why he cast Huppert, Russell sums it up this way: "She's serious, intense, French and very sexy. She's practically a legend in France, and has the most impeccable style and taste, but she's also willing to have her face be slammed in the mud."

"Everyone who worked on this film wonders what it is about," admits Huppert. "But there's so much going on in the movie, you can't really put it into words. I would say it is a modern fable about our modern world, and about how people have such different views of how to get along inside it."

She got a kick out of her distinctly European character. "Basically, Lily Tomlin and Dustin Hoffman think that everything is meant to happen, and my character believes the opposite. They think positive, I think negative. They are American. I am French. And I want to take my revenge on them," she summarizes.

As a veteran of numerous international films with many of the world's most influential directors, Huppert was drawn to David O. Russell as an iconoclast. "He has his own vision," she observes. "In this movie, nothing is predictable. I believe if things are predictable, then it's not a good sign. For me, the unpredictability of the film made it a totally compelling experience."

The film also boasts a wide array of talent in supporting and cameo roles including Tippi Hedren, who was discovered by Alfred Hitchcock and starred in such classics as *The Birds* and *Marnie*, playing Mary Jane Hutchinson, an enthusiastic member of Albert's Open Spaces Coalition. Kevin Dunn (*Mississippi Burning, Hot Shots*) plays Marty, the General Manager at Huckabees, who wants only the best for his company even if it means replacing his star employees. Also making a cameo is country western singing sensation Shania Twain, who is the key to Brad's plan for the Open Spaces black-tie benefit.

Rounding out the cast are Talia Shire (*Rocky* films and *The Godfather* trilogy), who plays Albert's mother, Mrs. Silver, and is, in fact, Schwartzman's mother in real life; Bob Gunton (*The Shawshank Redemption*) as Mr. Silver; Jean Smart (*Designing Women*) as the compassionate Mrs. Hooten; Dustin Hoffman's son Jake Hoffman in the role of the valet; David O. Russell's son Matthew Grillo-Russell, who plays one of the Mancala Hour game players, and David O. Russell's mother-in-law Angela Grillo, who plays Councilwoman Angela Franco.

CAST AND CREW CREDITS

FOX SEARCHLIGHT PICTURES Presents

In association with QWERTY FILMS

A KANZEON / SCOTT RUDIN / N1 EUROPEAN FILM PRODUKTIONS Production

DUSTIN HOFFMAN   ISABELLE HUPPERT   JUDE LAW   JASON SCHWARTZMAN

LILY TOMLIN   MARK WAHLBERG   NAOMI WATTS

"I ♥ HUCKABEES"

KEVIN DUNN   TIPPI HEDREN   BOB GUNTON

| Casting by | Music by | Co-Producer | Costume Designer |
| MARY VERNIEU, CSA | JON BRION | DARA L. WEINTRAUB | MARK BRIDGES |

| Film Editor | Production Designer | Director of Photography | Executive Producer |
| ROBERT K. LAMBERT, A.C.E. | K.K. BARRETT | PETER DEMING, ASC | MICHAEL KUHN |

Produced by
DAVID O. RUSSELL   GREGORY GOODMAN   SCOTT RUDIN

Written by
DAVID O. RUSSELL & JEFF BAENA

Directed by
DAVID O. RUSSELL

CAST

Albert Markovski . . . . JASON SCHWARTZMAN
Caterine Vauban . . . . ISABELLE HUPPERT
Bernard . . . . DUSTIN HOFFMAN
Vivian . . . . LILY TOMLIN
Brad Stand . . . . JUDE LAW
Tommy Corn . . . . MARK WAHLBERG
Dawn Campbell . . . . NAOMI WATTS
Angela Franco . . . . ANGELA GRILLO
Mr. Nimieri . . . . GER DUANY
Darlene . . . . DARLENE HUNT
Marty . . . . KEVIN DUNN
Davy . . . . BENNY HERNANDEZ
Josh . . . . RICHARD APPEL
Harrison . . . . BENJAMIN NURICK
Tim . . . . JAKE MUXWORTHY
Bobby . . . . PABLO DAVANZO
Construction Worker . . . . MATTHEW MUZIO
Firemen . . . . SHAWN PATRICK
PATRICK WALSH
Mary Jane Hutchinson . . . . TIPPI HEDREN
Frosh Girls . . . . ASHLEY A. FONDREVAY
LISA GUZMAN
Bik Schottinger . . . . SCOTT WANNBERG
Mrs. Echevarria . . . . ALTAGRACIA GUZMAN
Translator . . . . SAID TAGHMAOUI
Mrs. Hooten . . . . JEAN SMART

Cricket . . . . SYDNEY ZARP
Bret . . . . JONAH HILL
Orrin Spence . . . . DENIS HAYES
Boy At Mancala Hour . . . MATTHEW GRILLO-RUSSELL
Boy's Mother . . . . JANET GRILLO
Security Guards . . . . ADAM CLINTON
. . . . ANTONIO EVANS
Daryl . . . . ROBERT LAMBERT
Heather . . . . ISLA FISHER
Corporate Board . . . . KIMBERLY CUTTER
JOHN ROTHMAN
Mrs. Silver . . . . TALIA SHIRE
Mr. Silver . . . . BOB GUNTON
Molly Corn . . . . KAMALA LOPEZ-DAWSON
Caitlin Corn . . . . SAIGE RYAN CAMPBELL
Turkish Man . . . . KAIED HUSSAN
Dexicorp Attorney . . . . CHUCK SAFTLER
Medic . . . . JAMES J. MCCOY (PERIOD ADDED)
Shania Twain . . . . AS HERSELF
Formal Couple . . . . GEORGE MEYER
MARIA SEMPLE
Corporate Man . . . . JERRY SCHUMACHER
Ladies In Gowns . . . . JULIE ANN JOHNSON
JEANNIE EPPER-KIMACK
Maitre'd . . . . KEITH BARRETT
Valet . . . . JAKE HOFFMAN

Stunt Coordinator	BEN BRAY
Stunt Players	RAY SIEGLE
	DANNY DOWNEY
	TOM DEWIER
	ANNE CHATTERTON
	JOEY BOX
	SEAN GRAHAM
Unit Production Manager	DARA L. WEINTRAUB
First Assistant Director	MARY ELLEN WOODS
Second Assistant Director . .	SALLY SUE BEISEL-LANDER
Supervising Sound Editor	KELLY OXFORD M.P.S.E.
Re-Recording Mixers	RICK ASH
	ADAM JENKINS
Production Executives for N1 and Qwerty Films	
	MALCOLM RITCHIE
	JILL TANDY
For N1	PETER LÜKE
Executive in Charge of Production for N1 . .	MARK WOLFE
Music Supervisor	CREATIVE LICENSE
Production Supervisor	KIMBERLY L. RACH
2nd 2nd Assistant Director	JODI LOWRY-FISHER
Script Supervisor	KAREN GOLDEN
Camera Operator	LOU WEINERT
First Assistant A Camera	SCOTT RESSLER
Second Assistant A Camera	LISA K. FERGUSON
B Camera Operators	HENRY CLINE
	AMY VINCENT
First Assistant B Camera	DAVID EUBANK
Loaders	PAUL TILDEN
	MICHELLE BAKER
Steadicam Operators	BOB GORELICK
	CHRIS SQUIRES
Camera Intern	KYLE JEWELL
Video Engineer	DAVE DEEVER
Still Photographer	CLAUDETTE BARIUS
Art Director	SETH REED
Set Designer	LYNN CHRISTOPHER
Graphic Designer	WILLIAM ELISCU
Art Department Coordinator	KATHERINE WILSON
Art Department Production Assistant . . .	CALE WILBANKS
Production Coordinator	MIKE HUBERT
Assistant Coordinator	JENNIFER KERN
Production Secretaries	DMITRI VIGNESWAREN
	SUZANNE LEHFELDT
Production Accountant	R. BRADLEY DAVIS
1st Assistant Accountant	ROBERT LANE

Payroll Accountant	CINDY NEVINS
2nd Assistant Accountant	KIMBERLI STRETCH
Accounting Clerk	ANTHONY ALLEGRE
Post Production Accountant . .	R.C. BARAL & COMPANY
Key Grip	PHILIP M. SLOAN
Best Boy Grip	PAUL WILKOWSKY
Dolly Grip	TIMOTHY COLLINS
Grips	RICHARD KUHN
	DOUGLAS DOLE
	MARK VOLLMER
	DENNIS KUNEFF
	GARY LOUZON
	GENE B. KERRY
	CLIFF SPERRY
Gaffer	MICHAEL LA VIOLETTE
Best Boy Electric	ERIC SANDLIN
Electricians	KEN SYLVESTER
	MICHAEL JENKINS
	PAUL POSTAL
Location Manager	JIM MACEO
Key Assistant Location Manager . . .	PETER MARTORANO
Assistant Location Manager	GUY MORRISON
Location Scouts	QUENTIN HALLIDAY
	MICHAEL BREWER
	TYLER ELLIOTT
Post Production Supervisor	TIM PEDEGANA
Additional Editing	MARK BOURGEOIS
	PAMELA MARCH
Assistant Editors	RONALD WHITE
	JUSTIN C. GREEN
Editorial Assistant	DARWIN GREEN
Visual Effects Supervisor	RUSSELL BARRETT
Visual Effects Producer	SCOTT PUCKETT
Lead Visual Effects Artist	JOE KASTELY
Supervising Sound Assistant	VICTOR RAY ENNIS
Sound Design	TIM WALSTON M.P.S.E.
	MICHAEL KAMPER
Dialogue Editors	LAURA HARRIS
	CHRIS HOGAN M.P.S.E.
	TIM KIMMEL
ADR Editors	JAY KEISER
	JULIE FEINER
Sound Assistant	PAUL FLINCHBAUGH
Foley Recordist	MICHAEL McNERNEY
Foley Artist	JAMES BAILEY
Voice Casting by	CAITLIN McKENNA

Re-Recorded at
TODD AO STUDIOS WEST

Todd AO ADR Mixer. . . . . GREG STEELE
Todd AO ADR Recordist . . . . . CHRIS FITZGERALD
Todd AO Mix Technician . . .*. . . . . . . MARK HARRIS
POP Sound ADR Mixer . . . . . . MICHAEL S. MILLER
POP Sound ADR Recordist . . . . . COURTNEY BISHOP

Sound Editing by. . . . . SOUNDELUX

Additional Visual Effects by
HOWARD ANDERSON CO.

Executive Producer . . . . BOBBY BELL
Visual Effects Producer . . . . JONATHAN STERN
Senior Digital Artist . . . . PETER C. KOCZERA
Lead Digital Artist . . . . SHANNON NOBLE
Supervisor of Technology . . . . BOB MICHELETTI
Compositing Artists . . . . DEREK LEDBETTER
STEVE FAGERQUIST
DAVE FEINNER
CHRISTOPHER GRANDEL
Scanning and Recording Technician . . . . . . JOHN PAYNE
Digital Color Timer . . . . HILARY MURRAY
Line-up/Editorial. . . . . MIKE GRIFFIN
RICHARD EBERHARDT
Data Manager . . . . FRED JIMENEZ
Production Coordinator . . . . MANNY SIDA
Senior Staff . . . . HECTOR BITAR
Title Artist . . . . CHARLES McDONALD

Production Sound Recorder . . . . EDWARD TISE
Boom Operator . . . . ALBERT AQUINO
Cable Operator . . . . GEORGE FLORES

Music Editor . . . . JONATHAN KARP
Score Recorded and Mixed by . . . . TOM BILLER
Additional Engineer . . . . ERIC CAUDIEUX
Assistant Engineer . . . . DAN MONTI
Musician Contractor . . . . DEBBI DATZ-PYLE
Score Recorded at . . . . THE VILLAGE RECORDER

Choreographer . . . . MICHAEL ROONEY

Dialect Coach . . . . CARLA MEYER

Costume Supervisor . . . . PAUL H. LOPEZ
Key Costumer . . . . HOLLY DAVIS
On Set Costumers . . . . LISA A. DOYLE
NANCY COLLINI
ANNIE LAOPARADONCHAI
Costumer . . . . SABINE HUBER
Office Coordinator . . . . THAO T.VU
Fitter-Cutter/Tailor . . . . MICHAEL TERESCHUK
Wardrobe Production Assistant . . . . . . SHERRY WALSH

Department Head Make Up . . . . DEBBIE ZOLLER
Key Make Up . . . . FELICIA LINSKY
Assistant Make Up . . . . DAVID DE LEON
Prosthetics . . . . HOWARD BERGER

Department Head Hair . . . . GAIL RYAN
Key Hair Stylist . . . . MARLENE WILLIAMS
Additional Hair . . . . LAUREL VAN DYKE

Property Master . . . . SEAN MANNION
Assistant Property Masters . . . . AMELIA DRAKE
KAREN BRUCK
JEANNE MARIE KUKOR
NOEL McCARTHY

Set Decorator . . . . GENE SERDENA
Leadman . . . . GRANT SAMSON
On Set Dresser . . . . CHRISTIAN KASTNER
Buyer . . . . ROBERT L. STOVER
Swing Gang . . . . MICHAEL GLYNN
MIKE BOUDREAU
JAMIE FLEMING
BOBBY POLLARD

Construction Coordinator . . . . CHRIS FORSTER
Construction Foreman . . . . ANDERS RUNDBLAD
Labor Foreman . . . . EDDIE ACUÑA
Gangbosses . . . . DARON SMITH
CHRIS LEE
Propmakers . . . . GREGORY PAUL AUSTIN
PHIL LAYMON
SCOTT HEAD
Laborer . . . . MANUEL HERNANDEZ
Paint Foreman . . . . KIP SAWYER
Lead Painter . . . . ERIC REICHARDT
On Set Painter . . . . LEE STEVEN ROSS
Paint Laborer . . . . ALEJANDRO POLI
Painter/Decorator . . . . PAULETTE FOX
Greensmen . . . . PORFIRIO SILVA
JESS ANSCOTT

Special Effects Coordinator . . . . MARTY BRESIN
Special Effects Foremen . . . . JEFF BRESIN
DALE ETTEMA

Transportation Coordinator . . . . AARON SKALKA
Transportation Captain . . . . KEITH FISHER

Unit Publicist . . . . PAULETTE DAUBER

Clearance Coordinator . . . . ASHLEY KRAVITZ

Casting Associate . . . . SHALIMAR REODICA
Casting Assistant . . . . VENUS KANANI
Extras Casting . . . . SANDE ALESSI

Catering Company . . . . MARIO'S CATERING
Chef. . . . . JAMIE TRUJILLO
Craft Service . . . . NICK MESTRANDREA
Craft Service Assistant . . . . TERRY PAINOVICH

Set Medic. . . . . ANTONIO EVANS
Construction Medics . . . . JONAS MATZ
DAVE FULTON
Security . . . . CAST SECURITY
Security Coordinator. . . . . EDDIE VELLANOWETH, JR

Negative Cutter . . . . MO HENRY
D. BASSETT & ASSOCIATES
Color Timer . . . . MATEOS DERAVANESSIAN
Film Dailies by . . . . FOTOKEM
Preview Engineer. . . . . LEE TUCKER

Assistants to David O. Russell . . . .
DUSTIN THOMAS CARTMILL
BRAD BAENA
Executive Assistants to Scott Rudin . . . . BEN HOWE
MIKE LAROCCA
ALEX FRATAR
Assistants To Scott Rudin . . . . JULES EGGLI
JON SILK
CONNOR PRICE
Assistant to Dara L. Weintraub . . . . . ERIC L. FERSTEN
Assistant to Mark Wahlberg . . . . ERIC WEINSTEIN
Assistant to Jason Schwartzman. . . . MERRITT JOHNSON
Assistants to Isabelle Huppert. . . . . AUSTIN FORMATO
JONATHAN NEWHALL
Assistants to Dustin Hoffman. . . . . AIMEE NANCE
STEVE DEMKO
Assistant to Lily Tomlin . . . . BOBBIE BLYLE
Assistants to Jude Law. . . . . BEN JACKSON
MIKE LUND
BENJAMIN RIGAUD
Assistants to Naomi Watts. . . . . ANNALIESE LEVY
KAISER CLARK
Office Production Assistants . . . . AMY LYDDY
CHRIS SLOAN
BRANDON HOWE
Key Set Production Assistant . . . . ALEX LEIMONE
Set Production Assistants . . . . FALLON JOHNSON
CORY HALL
NICHOLAS FITZGERALD
PAULIE STENERSON
CHAMONIX BOSCH

FOR QWERTY FILMS
Head of Commercial and Business Affairs . . . .
ANDREW HILDEBRAND
Head of Legal Affairs . . . . KATHRYN CRAIG
Chief Financial Officer . . . . MARK WOOLLEY

Production Coordinator . . . . SARAH NUTTALL
Assistant to Mr. Kuhn . . . . . . ALEXANDRA ARLANGO

U.K. Legal Counsel . . . .
RICHARD PHILIPPS, RICHARDS BUTLER

Post Production Consultant on behalf of N1 . . . .
STEVE HARROW

Collection Account Management . . . . . FINTAGE HOUSE

"MAN! I FEEL LIKE A WOMAN!"
WRITTEN BY SHANIA TWAIN AND ROBERT JOHN LANGE
PERFORMED BY SHANIA TWAIN
COURTESY OF MERCURY RECORDS UNDER
LICENSE FROM UNIVERSAL MUSIC ENTERPRISES

"BEETHOVEN'S STRING QUARTET #14, OP. 151"
PERFORMED BY THE KODALY QUARTET
COURTESY OF NAXOS
BY ARRANGEMENT WITH SOURCE/Q

Score material based on the following songs:
Didn't Think It Would Turn Out Bad
Wouldn't Have It Any Other Way
Revolving Door
Over Our Heads
Strangest Times
JB's Blues
I Get What It's About
You Learn True To Yourself
Ska
Monday
You Can't Take It With You
all songs written by Jon Brion

Musicians
Harp - Katie Kirkpatrick
Flutes - Jim Walker
Euphonium - Bill Reichenbach
Upright Bass - Sebastian Steinberg
String Quartet - Eric Gorfaine
Daphne Chen
Leah Katz
Richard Dodd
All other instruments - Jon Brion
Mighty Wurlitzer courtesy of John Ledwon
Score Collages - Jonathan Karp
Music Consultant - Christine Bergren

THE PRODUCERS WISH TO THANK:
JOHN LESHER
JANET GRILLO
LUKE BOURGEOIS
PABLO DAVANZO

ALAN DRESSLER
ARI EMANUEL
CHAD GRIFFIN
KEVIN KELLY
LANTANA
PETER LEVINE
JEFF MANDELL
ADAM MCKAY
ALEXANDER PAYNE
THE LOST BOYS FOUNDATION
KIM PIERCE
SHIRA PIVEN
BRUCE RAMER
RANDY SCHNITMAN
ROBERT THURMAN
SHANIA TWAIN
ACHILLES
DIANE UPSON
PRADA
CHRISTIAN LOUBOUTIN
CRÈME DE LA MER
EIDC LOS ANGELES FILM OFFICE
CREATIVE MEDIA MARKETING
CALIFORNIA FILM COMMISSION
POOLE
CITY OF TORRANCE
KAI
CITY OF HERMOSA BEACH

STOCK PHOTOGRAPHY PROVIDED BY
CORBIS IMAGES

TM/©2004 FAMILY OF BABE RUTH AND THE BABE
RUTH LEAGUE, INC. BY CMG WORLDWIDE INC.
WWW.BABERUTH.COM

ELVIS PRESLEY'S IMAGE AND LIKENESS COURTESY
OF ELVIS PRESLEY ENTERPRISES, INC.

N1 EUROPEAN FILM PRODUKTIONS -GMBH & CO.
KG IS THE AUTHOR OF THIS MOTION PICTURE FOR
PURPOSES OF COPYRIGHT AND OTHER LAWS.

Lighting Equipment by
PASKAL LIGHTING

Camera Cranes by
CHAPMAN / LEONARD STUDIO EQUIPMENT, INC.

Cranes and Dollies by
J. L. FISHER

Camera Equipment by
PANAVISION

Film by
EASTMAN KODAK

Film by
FUJI

Color by Deluxe

The events, characters and firms depicted in this motion picture
are fictitious. Any similarity to actual persons, living or dead, or
to actual events or firms is purely coincidental.

RELEASED BY TWENTIETH CENTURY FOX
(FOX TERRITORIES)

BIOGRAPHIES

DAVID O. RUSSELL (Director/Producer/Writer)

David O. Russell's first feature, *Spanking The Monkey*, premiered at the 1994 Sundance Film Festival where it won the Audience Award. The film also earned Russell Independent Spirit Awards for Best First Feature and Best First Screenplay.

1996 saw the release of Russell's acclaimed comedy *Flirting With Disaster*, which appeared on more than thirty critics' Top Ten lists and garnered Independent Spirit Award nominations for Russell for Best Director and Best Screenplay.

Three Kings was named to more than one hundred critics' Top Ten lists when it was released in 1999. Amongst the many accolades received, the Boston Critics Association awarded the film Best Feature and Russell Best Director. Russell was also nominated for a Writers Guild of America Award for Best Original Screenplay. *Three Kings* has been recently re-released theatrically and on DVD with a short documentary featuring war veterans as they return home.

In 2002, Russell was the first director honored by The New York Museum of Modern Art's series "Works in Progress" which focuses on a new generation of filmmakers, and has since honored Alexander Payne and Sofia Coppola.

JEFF BAENA (Co-Writer)

I ♥ Huckabees marks Jeff Baena's first produced screenplay. A native of Miami, Baena attended New York University where he studied screenwriting and directing. He is currently working on several projects including his directorial debut with Fox Searchlight.